—Western Collection, Denver Public Library

COLORADO'S UNIQUE NARROW-GAUGE

the Gilpin Gold Tram

COLORADO'S UNIQUE NARROW-GAUGE

Mallory Hope Ferrell

PRUETT PUBLISHING COMPANY

Boulder, Colorado

Acknowledgments

No author writes a book all by himself, especially if the subject concerns our American West. There are the many characters who "played the parts," whether or not they realized it at the time. Then there are those who recorded the events with ink or upon glass plates, and finally those who had the foresight to preserve faded photographs and records.

The Gilpin Gold Tram is no exception. I am indebted to a number of individuals for their help, encouragement and cooperation. The artwork on these pages is mainly from the pen and brush of two of the finest railroad illustrators in the business: Howard Fogg of Boulder, Colorado and M. W. Holtzinger of Norfolk, Virginia. Not only do they know their art, but they know their trains, too.

Photographs of the Gilpin Tramway have always been rare and much sought-after collectors' items. Until recent years only a handful of good tramway pictures had been turned up. Two years ago a concerted effort was made to track down and copy all of the existing photographs of the tramway. The result of this search by many different historical hunters is displayed on the following pages. Special thanks for taking part in the "hunt" go to Richard B. Jackson,

Richard H. Kindig, Opal Harber of the Denver Public Library's Western Collection, Kay Pierson and Enid Thompson of the State Historical Society of Colorado, Dave Rees, Edward Bond and members of Denver's scale model group, the "Dirty Dozen."

Jon MacNeil was especially helpful with his fine collection of photographs and data from old Central City newspapers. The last-minute discovery of a rare collection of Gilpin Tramway paper items by Robert W. Richardson of the Colorado Railroad Museum helped to fill a void in that area.

Scale drawings by John E. Robinson and the late H. Temple Crittenden were carefully researched and accurately drawn especially for this book.

The fine cooperation displayed by Fred A. Pruett and his Western History Editor, Gerald Keenan, made the production stages of this book a real pleasure. One last word of thanks to my son, Mallory III, who was a great companion on hiking trips over the old grades, carrying those peanut butter sandwiches and four-by-five film holders. I am deeply indebted to all of these people, and sincerely hope the book is worthy of their efforts.

4

Dedication

He was a fine model builder, master draftsman, historian and author, but most of all H. Temple Crittenden was a good friend who was always willing to share his research. I had the rare opportunity to grow up in Henry's shadow, only a few miles from his white frame Virginia home. It was there, as a kid, that I first learned about valve gears and Shay locomotives. The scale drawings in this tome are the final work of the most noted two-foot-gauge authority of our time, the ore car drawings were completed only hours before his passing. His many books about narrow-gauge railroads are a significant contribution for the historians of the future, and the dedication of this book to Henry is only a small way of saying "thanks" to an old friend.

The Gilpin Tram with clanking gears,
The call of the ore in those golden years;
Snorting along on tortuous grades,
Manned by men well hep to their trade.
Shuttling pay dirt from mine to mill,
Barely enough income to pay the bill.
Maintenance was high on the rolling stock
That finally led to the auction block.
Together the mines and tram died out,
A calamity to the camp, no doubt.
Together they faded into the past
The end of whistle and dynamite blast.
Ghosts now revel in abandoned mines,
O'er the old railroad the blizzard whines.
Gone are they that manned the train,
Gone forever the glorious twain.

—GUS GRUTZMACHER

Foreword

In Colorado, a state noted for its twisting narrow-gauge rails and steep grades, the Gilpin Tramway was unique. Not only was it narrow-gauge, but it was the only two-foot-wide railroad in a land renowned for yard-wide trackage.

The "tram," as it was known locally, was constructed for the sole purpose of hauling ore from the mines of the "Little Kingdom of Gilpin" to the ore-processing mills clustered along North Clear Creek in Black Hawk. Built in an era when gold was extracted from beneath Quartz Hill by bearded miners with seven-pound hammers, star drills and sheer determination, the tram lasted as long as the mines justified its existence.

In the 1880's, the difference between a gold mine and "just another lode" was transportation. The tram put an end to exorbitant teaming costs and provided a means of economically converting low-grade ore into precious metal.

Light rails separated by only twenty-four inches supported Shay-geared locomotives and diminutive cars over some of the steepest grades and sharpest turns in the West. The Gilpin Tram twisted and clawed its way up to the mines on tracks that clung to the side of mountains and hung on man-made rock shelves. In its final years, the tram was owned and operated by the Colorado and Southern, but even "the Colorado Road" could not foresee nor forstall the decline in mining, and the little line came to an end on the eve of World War I.

Some of the glory of the tram can be realized by hiking over the abandoned grades, across tumbled-down bridges, through deep rock cuts and up the eroding switchbacks. On a sunny day the old grade still sparkles with the glint of precious ores that once rode down to the smelters in one-cord cars. Much of the right-of-way remains virtually intact, even after more than a half-century of disuse.

Today the Gilpin Tramway is preserved in fading old photographs, yellowing waybills, an occasional spike picked up on Banta Hill and . . . memories. Here then is the tramway's story: its sunny days, the air filled with the scent of soft coal and Shay valve oil, to the bitter blizzards that struck with paralyzing regularity—here she comes!

Time Table

Foreword   6

1. Sparkle In The Pan   9

2. From Mine To Mill   19

3. Running The Tram   37

4. The Colorado Road Takes Over   59

5. Gilpin Ghost   85

6. Links and Pins   91

Index   108

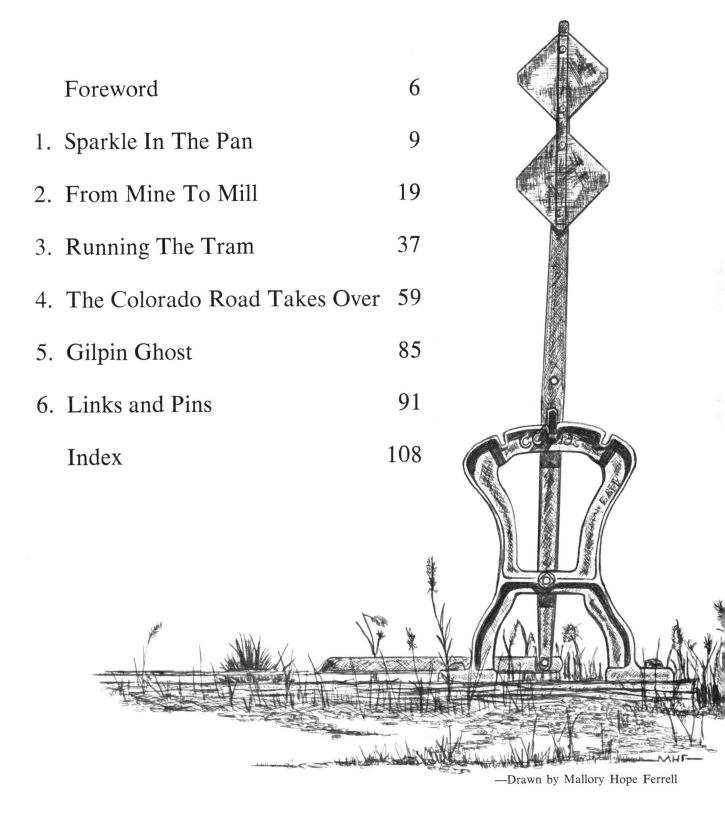

—Drawn by Mallory Hope Ferrell

CASEY
HOLTZINGER

Sparkle in the Pan

Early in 1858 the Russell brothers, with a party of nine men, left the declining Georgia gold fields, intent on finding new wealth in the Rocky Mountains. Six miles above Denver, at a place called Montana Diggins, they saw pay dirt. When the Russell party returned to the Missouri River for supplies, the news of their discovery started a mad rush for the Rockies. This rush was generally known as the Pike's Peak Gold Rush; although that mountain was a full sixty miles away, it was considered close enough by the plainsmen in their Conestoga wagons however, and the rallying cry of "Pike's Peak Or Bust" was heard across the nation.

The next point of discovery was on what is now Clear Creek, due west of the present city of Golden, Colorado. In April, 1859, John H. Gregory and a companion started upstream, panning for gold. At the fork of the creek they took the north branch and found the richest gold dust in what is now Gregory Gulch, above Black Hawk.

Returning to Denver City, Gregory guided a party of twelve men to the new find, taking four days to make the trip. On May 6, 1859, the Gregory Lode was discovered, the first pan of dirt yielding $4 in gold. Other discoveries followed in quick succession.

The Bates Lode was located on May 15th and the Smith on the 20th, followed two days later by the Dean and Castro finds. The Gunnell, Kansas and Burroughs Lodes high atop Quartz Hill were found on the 25th; many other ore bodies were claimed by the first week of June.

During the first seven days at the original Gregory Lode, five men gleaned $1,914 in gold dust and nuggets from the sluice boxes. A month after the first strike, there were more than one hundred sluices operating in Gregory Gulch, paying an average of $30 per man each day.

On May 16th, 1859 the first mining district was organized, limiting the size of a lode claim. This was to be a great drawback in later years, and was eventually overcome by the consolidation of the various properties.

By the end of September the population of the district had risen to over nine-hundred. The residents lived in crude log shanties and tents. Storekeepers came up from the plains and set up shop near the diggings. By the year's end, the new camp had produced almost a million dollars in gold. The figures become more impressive when you consider that the entire district was only about two and a half miles wide by four miles long.

In the summer of 1860 there were sixty mills and thirty arastras in operation, and the population had risen to 15,000. Many of these stamp mills were of primitive design, with wood stems fitted with ox shoes and strap iron to crush the ore. Arastras crushed the softer surface ore and were run by oxen or water power. At best, the process of extracting gold from the ore was crude and inefficient. However, the unrefined mills brought returns of $60 to $100 per ton, an indication of the high grade of ore being processed.

The news of the Gregory diggings soon caught the eye of Eastern speculators, and a wild era of stock gambling ensued. Many of the mines passed into the ownership of capitalists in far-off Boston, New York and Baltimore during the Civil War. The period was marked by more stock exchanging than actual mining, but people continued to arrive as each day passed.

With the large influx of population in the mid-sixties, there was simply not enough ground to go around, and so the miners scattered out over the nearby hills, making new discoveries in the

Central City was a thriving boom town when George D. Wakely made this photograph from atop Central Hill in 1864. The buildings were constructed of wood, and were destroyed in a great fire ten years later.

process. Mining camps sprang up overnight in typical "gold rush" fashion. Soon the settlements of Nevadaville, Russell Gulch, Central, Apex, and Black Hawk were fighting for leadership in the emerging district. At first, buildings were little more than tents with wooden floors and false fronts, but the inevitable fire that seemed to follow gold fever to every mining camp soon proved the practical advantages of stone and brick construction.

Black Hawk and Central City were granted charters by the Territorial Legislature in 1864.

Central City was virtually destroyed by a fire ten years later. The fire reputedly was started by one of the many Chinese miners who lived in wooden shanties along what is now Spring Street. The celestial was lighting his joss papers to say his prayers when the conflagration started. The granite walls of the Teller House and the Register building across the street were all that stopped the fire from leveling the camp.

The natural topography of Gilpin County dictated the location of the mills. Reduction works required great amounts of water and the

Black Hawk was the location of smelters and mills for the Gilpin gold strike. The first smelter was built by Professor Nathaniel P. Hill in 1867. —Harry Lake

only dependable supply was along the North Fork of Clear Creek in Black Hawk. The town took its name from the Blackhawk Mining Company, which in turn used the name of a popular brand of mining machinery.

It was here in Black Hawk that Professor Nathaniel P. Hill built the first smelter in Colorado in 1867. The original smelter was capable of producing twelve tons of concentrate daily and it commenced operations in January, 1868. Within a few years, mills and smelters lined North Clear Creek for several miles. Professor Hill was later to serve as mayor of Black Hawk, and as United States senator after the territory became a state in 1876.

The gold pan and sluice box of the early 1860's gave way to the star drill and seven-pound hammer as the surface ore was exhausted. There was still gold dust in the creek beds, but the real lodes were buried deep under the mountains. By 1875 there were twenty-two stamp mills in the district with an aggregate of four-hundred and forty stamps, and by the autumn of the following year, the air resounded to the sound of seven hundred and seventy stamps dropping on gold-bearing ore day and night.

Transportation of the ores became a problem as soon as hard rock mining came into vogue. The crude paths used by the grinding ore wagons could hardly be called roads. They were clogged with mud in the spring, filled with dust in summer and fall, and packed with snow during the winter months. The cursing teamsters brought down wagons loaded with a quarter-ton of quartz using mules, sweat and determination. The high teaming cost shut down many low-grade mines. The first road known to have been built in the district was constructed from Quartz Hill to Black Hawk in 1860. Two years later a teamster named Casey built a wagon road from Gregory Gulch to Chase Gulch.

As early as 1865 the all-powerful Union Pacific Railroad had encouraged the Colorado & Clear Creek Railroad to construct a line from Denver and Golden though the Rocky Mountains to Brigham Young's Salt Lake City. The plan failed when the Union Pacific decided to build its mainline through Cheyenne, far to the north. Some grading was accomplished from the Territorial Capital of Golden in the early part of 1868. The project remained trackless until the Union Pacific realized that Denver was soon to be the railhead of both the Kansas Pacific and the Denver Pacific railroads, each laying standard gauge trackage toward the Queen City of the Plains. In 1870, the Union Pacific helped reorganize the old Colorado & Clear Creek line into the Colorado Central Rail Road Company. That year, trackage was spiked down between Golden and Denver, arriving just after the Denver Pacific and Kansas Pacific rails had arrived.

In 1873 Jay Gould gained control over the Union Pacific and began construction of the Colorado Central Rail Road from Golden to Cheyenne, thus paralleling the Denver Pacific Railway. Under Gould's command, the Union Pacific refused to interchange freight with the Kansas Pacific Railway or the Denver Pacific Railway, making them, eventually, so financially weak that the Union Pacific was able to absorb them.

Early in 1872 construction was started by the Colorado Central on a three-foot-gauge line from Golden to the booming mining towns in the mountains. Taking a page from the book of General William Jackson Palmer and his success with three-foot-gauge on the Denver & Rio Grande, Colorado Central President W. A. H. Loveland selected yard-wide trackage for his mountain lines.

Three small Porter Bell & Company 0-4-0 tender locomotives, reportedly from a little-known wharf operation of the Union Pacific Railroad at Omaha, were sent to Golden for construction of the line to Black Hawk. Ten flatcars were also sent to the narrow-gauge division of the Colorado Central. Later one of the flatcars was rebuilt into a passenger car, while three others became boxcars. Little is known of the construction locomotives; they do not appear on the first Colorado Central roster nor in the numbering system of that road. One old stereo view at Elk Meadow in 1872 however, clearly shows an 0-4-0 at the head of a construction train.

On December 15, 1872 the Colorado Central was completed into Black Hawk. The new mining district now had a connection with the rest of the world and a means of getting the gold shipments to Denver.

In February, 1872, the Central City *Daily Register* advised:

> The Gilpin County Tram Railway Company is the name of a new organization whose object is to construct tram railways to various mines, thus facilitating the transportation of ore, fuel, etc. The company has as its head Mr. Leahy and Mr. Darcey, and we learn that they have sufficient backing to guarantee success. They hope to have a portion of their tramway completed by May first. The enterprise should be a paying one. It has our best wishes for its success.

By early July Edmond Leahy's men had completed grading from Black Hawk up North Clear Creek to near Mammoth Gulch. One mile of track was completed and the gauge was given as three feet, "uniform with our narrow-gauge railways." A white mule provided the motive power for this short-lived pole road. Trackage was completed for a distance of about seventeen miles to a spot known as Michigan Valley, at the headwaters of North Clear Creek. By 1873 the line was in debt, and in March of the following year the timber land in Michigan Valley was sold at public auction. The line was not designed for hauling gold but was a logging road, bringing down timber to the mines for shoring and to the mills for fuel and charcoal. The pole rails were actually pine logs six to eight inches in diameter and about sixteen feet long. These poles were set in stringers without the benefit of any metal spikes.

Normal operations on the original Gilpin County Tram saw two men load timber in the cutting area aboard the four-wheel cars and then coast down to Black Hawk with two cars chained together. The cars were unloaded and then hauled back to the timberland by a mule. The operation was not a success and in May, 1874 Leahy mortaged all he had, which was very little, ". . . . two mare mules, harness and a Schuttler wagon," for $250. The big Central City fire occured on May 21, 1874, and had the town been rebuilt with wood rather than brick, the ending for the Gilpin County Tram Railway Company might not have come so soon.

—HEY MULE
by M. W. Holtzinger

Slim Rails up Clear Creek

In 1870 the Colorado Central Rail Road constructed a standard-gauge line between the Territorial Capitol of Golden and Denver City. Two years later construction of a narrow-gauge line to the gold fields was begun. In the photograph (above) both narrow and standard gauge motive power fills the Golden roundhouse in this 1874 view. —Richard B. Jackson. At the right is a rare view of one of the Porter Bell & Company 0-4-0 tender locomotives used to construct the Clear Creek line, at Elk Meadow in 1872. —Richard B. Jackson. Below is a builder's photo of Colorado Central No. 4 as she came from the Porter Bell works in 1873. —Mallory Hope Ferrell.

The three-foot-gauge rails reached Black Hawk in 1872, and were extended by the use of switchbacks to Central City in 1878. Above, we find Colorado Central 2, a Porter Bell of 1875 poised on the Mountain City Trestle between Black Hawk and Central City soon after service started between the gold camps. —Charles Weitfle, State Historical Society of Colorado. An eastbound freight train (above right) brings down ore from the mines with engine 4 leading the way through Clear Creek Canyon. The 4 has had the saddle tank removed and now sports a small four-wheel tender. —State Historical Society of Colorado Collection. Below is Colorado Central 2 as she appeared in 1882 with pine boughs decorating her dome. —E. J. Haley Collection.

Colorado Central 1 leaves Central City with boxcar 10 and a coach in 1878, the year trackage was extended up Gregory Gulch from Black Hawk. —Charles Weitfle, author's collection.

Black Hawk was a thriving mill town by 1874, with smelters lining both sides of North Clear Creek, and the sounds of hundreds of stamps filling the evening air. —Charles Weitfle, State Historical Society of Colorado.

Excursions to the mountains west of Denver were popular summer attractions for many years. Above, a train load of tourists inspect a mine in Clear Creek Canyon in 1898. The four car train is headed by 109, a Union Pacific Denver & Gulf 2-8-0. Mining machinery bound for the Gilpin district from the east (left) had to be transferred from standard gauge cars to three foot gauge equipment at Denver or Golden and again reloaded onto the two foot gauge before final delivery to the mine.—Author's Collection

SHARES, $10.EACH.

CAPITAL STOCK $200.000.

SHARES
1300 5

THE GILPIN
Tramway Company

NUMBER
157

This is to Certify that *Frederick Kruse* is the owner of *Thirteen Hundred* Shares of Capital Stock of

The Gilpin Tramway Company, FULL PAID AND NON-ASSESSABLE, transferable only on the Books of the Company in person or by Attorney on surrender of this Certificate.

In Witness Whereof the said Company has caused this Certificate to be signed by its President and Secretary and its corporate seal to be affixed at Central City, Colo. this *October 7th* 18 *96*

_____ Secretary.   *Robert Williams* President.

CANCELLED   CANCELLED

INCORPORATED UNDER THE LAWS OF THE STATE OF COLORADO.

Geller & Cleveland Lith. Co., Denver, Colo.

20,000. SHARES.

Mine to Mill

CHAPTER 2

Gilpin County, the smallest in size in Colorado, is one of the richest in a state noted for its mineral wealth. The "Little Kingdom of Gilpin," as it is often called, helped to provide the economic foundation and attract the necessary population to gain statehood for the territory in 1876.

The three-foot-gauge Colorado Central Rail Road was extended from Black Hawk to Central City in 1878. The less-than-one mile between the two camps required slightly over four miles of trackage and two spectacular switchbacks to reach the county seat.

Now the blackjack dealers, miners, fancy ladies and hangers-on could ride in comfort from Denver to the very heart of the "Little Kingdom." Saloons lined both sides of Central City's Main Street, and Mack's Brewery was hard pressed to keep up with the demand for local beer. But there was still no dependable, economical means of transporting the gold-bearing quartz from the mines high above the thriving camps down to the mills.

In the summer of 1886 five mining men met with the intent to form a unique railroad. The Gilpin Tramway Company was organized on July 29th in Central City by Henry C. Bolsinger, Bradford H. Locke, Robert A. Campbell, Andrew W. Rogers and Henry J. Hawley. The stated purpose of the new company was to build a two-foot-gauge railroad to transport ore from the mines to the various mills and sampling works in Black Hawk.

The success of similar two-foot-gauge railroads in Maine probably prompted the selection of that gauge. The economic advantages of three-foot-gauge had been proven by the Denver & Rio Grande Railway in 1871 and copied by hundreds of other narrow-gauge roads across the nation. Howard Fleming's *Narrow Gauge Railways in America,* published in 1875, outlined the advantages to be gained from smaller equipment negotiating sharper curves and operating on steeper grades than was possible with rails spaced to the standard four-feet eight and a half inch width.

The Gilpin Tramway was the first and most famous two-foot-gauge common carrier in the West.

Capitalization of the Gilpin Tramway Company was set at $60,000, a sum which soon proved too little. A meeting was held on August 10, 1886, and Henry C. Bolsinger was named president, with Robert A. Campbell as secretary. Bolsinger was owner of the Hubert Mine, a major producer, while Campbell owned the Public Sampling Works in Black Hawk.

Bradford H. Locke was picked to build and manage the tram. His knowledge and engineering background were without peer in the region, but his ability to get along with business associates was practically nil. Brad Locke was always involved in one dispute or another. He was connected with the famous (some said "infamous") Slaughter House case which involved William Fullerton of the Gunnell Mine and the London-owned Josephine, managed by Locke. The suit was over the ownership of a rich plot of land on Quartz Hill, and while it went from one court to another the miners of the disputing firms were out of work. Years later, Locke showed up as manager of the Isabella Mine in Cripple Creek and was shortly run out of town by hostile miners when he attempted to lengthen the standard working day from eight to ten hours.

The first ten miles of the Gilpin Tramway were located as soon as the snows began to melt, and

◄ **Gilpin Tramway stock certificates are among the rarest of Colorado collector's items.** —Robert W. Richardson 19

Bradford Locke's crew is shown laying the original rails of the Gilpin Tramway up Chase Gulch in May, 1887. This was Colorado's first and only two-foot-gauge railroad. —Western Collection, Denver Public Library

20

Gilpin Tramway Shay 1, the "Gilpin." —Mallory Hope Ferrell Collection

grading was commenced in May, 1887. Eight miles of rail were on order, as well as a ten-ton Shay-geared locomotive and fourteen ore cars, from the Lima Locomotive & Machine Works of Lima, Ohio. The rail was thirty-five-pound iron from the Union Pacific's Utah & Northern Railway, which had converted, in July, 1887, its Pocatello, Idaho to Butte, Montana line from three-foot to standard-gauge, thus releasing a large quantity of light iron rail.

The tramway purchased a frame barn opposite the Sensenderfer residence on North Clear Creek in Black Hawk, covered the structure with sheet iron and began laying a foundation for shop machinery. This was the tram's first engine house and shop. A general office was maintained in a corner of the Colorado Central's depot in Central City.

The first rails were spiked into place on July 1, 1887 near the tram's depot grounds in upper Black Hawk. For the preceding month, Brad Locke had a large crew grading the switchbacks and building the high rock retaining walls in Chase Gulch. Track work was delayed due to lack of a locomotive. Shay 1, the "Gilpin," was shipped August 10th and arrived in Black Hawk aboard a flatcar on the 26th. The beautiful little engine was unloaded in front of Humphrey's Concentration Works as a crowd of town urchins looked on in excitement. By

noon the locomotive had been hauled down to the former barn-turned-Gilpin Tramway Company engine house for final assembly. On September 1st, the "Gilpin" was run about three-quarters of a mile and it was reported that the whistle could be clearly heard on Main Street in Central City.

September also saw the arrival of the first of fourteen steel ore cars from Lima. The tiny cars were sixteen feet long and four feet wide with eight fourteen inch wheels and a capacity of one-half cord. The cars weighed one and three-quarter tons each.

Just out of Black Hawk, it was necessary to blast a shelf for the eight-foot-wide roadbed. Near the Freedom Mill on Chase Gulch were several deep rock cuts. The thirty-five-pound iron rails were spiked to red spruce ties, four feet long and four inches square with sawed ends. The ties originally were spaced two feet on center. Maximum grade on the mainline was held to six percent and the minimum radius curve was sixty-six feet. There is, however, some indication that the line was originally built with several curves of fifty-foot radius. In later years, thirty-five-pound steel rails were used on ties measuring five feet long and five inches square.

Originally, wooden bridges were used across small creeks, but most of these were eventually

The "Gilpin" was photographed at the Lima Locomotive & Machine Works in Lima, Ohio just before she was shipped to Black Hawk, The small two-truck Shay had but two cylinders and weighed only ten tons. —P. E. Percy, Lima Collection

replaced by stone culverts. However, more than eighty years after their construction, a number of wooden bridges remain in place, a tribute to Locke's construction techniques. Long, wrought-iron spikes were driven into wooden timbers, then the cribbing was filled with stone.

As the tramway construction continued toward Nevadaville, the younger generation of Central City was out in force to watch the "kid-size" railroad in its progress. On September 29, 1887 the citizens of Gilpin were treated to a ride on the tram. The excursion train picked up a hundred people at the reservoir on upper Eureka Street and took them down to Black Hawk, where a tour was made of Mr. Fullerton's stamp mill. The ride back to Central City took but a half-hour. The train consisted of the "Gilpin" and five ore cars fitted with temporary seats. Specially constructed excursion cars were still a thing of the future for the tram.

A remarkable feature of the Gilpin Tramway was that it lacked a formal right-of-way. The line was built to the mines, and the mining men were happy enough to have the diminutive line. This informal arrangement did create a few problems, for the tram was not without its enemies.

An agreement was reached with the Colorado Central, then under Union Pacific control, to lay a third rail between the three-foot-gauge tracks, and the Colorado Central agreed to build to a point near the Hidden Treasure Mill in upper Black Hawk. This allowed the tram to lay a third rail between the Hidden Treasure and the Randolph Mills, approximately two miles. In return for this, the tramway directors said they would ship over the Colorado Central and would pay the bigger road $1,000 per year in rental.

Among those opposed to the new railroad was Black Hawk's Mayor William Fick. He fought the addition of a third rail on the Colorado Central through "his" town. It seems that the good mayor was closely tied with the teamsters, with whom the new two-foot-gauge line was in direct competition. The third rail was delayed by various legal actions until November 30, 1887, when Gilpin Tramway crews laid trackage below the Hidden Treasure, which was just inside the township. This allowed the tram to reach the Polar Star, Gregory, Bobtail and other mills below the mouth of Gregory Gulch.

The first ore shipment over the new Gilpin

The Gilpin Gets Going

The tramway's engine house (above) had originally seen service as a barn in upper Black Hawk, but served the two-foot-gauge well. The trestle in the foreground carried the mainline rails up Chase Gulch. Shay 1 arrived in Black Hawk on August 26, 1887 and was put to work at once (right) on a construction train. —S. L. Wells, Western Collection, Denver Public Library

Tram was made on December 11, 1887. The six-car train from the Grand Army shaft was delivered to the Meade Mill, another William Fullerton property. The Meade had a newly constructed switchback with a trestle over the ore bins. These bins were covered with sheet iron in order to protect them from possible sparks that might be dropped by the "Gilpin." By Christmas there was a regular train each day from the Grand Army to the Meade down on Clear Creek.

Two days after Christmas the "Gilpin" lost her footing behind the Mitchell residence above Second High Street. Engineer Starck received a few minor cuts and was discharged for careless running. Eighteen-year-old fireman Walter Beebe jumped, but dislocated his ankle. Several others sitting on the pilot beam escaped injury. A simultaneous call for help went out to Dr. Richmond and to the boys at the Eureka Foundry. Shay 1 was back in regular service before month's end.

The new year of 1888 saw the Gilpin Tramway completed to Nevadaville with enough rail on hand for an additional five miles.

When it was necessary to gain altitude, the tram resorted to the use of switchbacks; the trackage zig-zagged back and forth across the face of the mountain, avoiding sharp curves, high trestles and expensive tunneling. The tram had more switchbacks than any other American railroad; in one instance, seven switchbacks were used to reach just one mine. The very fact that there were so many switchbacks made disastrous runaways a rare occurrence. Ore cars spotted at the various mines occasionally got away and scattered their contents all over the mountainside, but usually the runaway cars lost their momentum on the tail end of a switchback and thus avoided an accident.

On January 6, 1888, a car of ore being unloaded at the Hidden Treasure Mill did get away and crashed into a wagon loaded with wood, at the Meade Mill. George Miller, who was unloading the wood, saw the car coming and jumped, but the ore car ground the wagon to splinters, killed one mule and hurt another. The ore car then struck another two-foot-gauge car hard enough to release the brakes, and the two loaded cars demolished a three-foot-gauge boxcar before coming to a halt opposite the Polar Star Mill in downtown Black Hawk.

In February, track crews were laying rails in Illinois Gulch, on the eastern slope of Quartz Hill, heading for the California Mine. Business was so good that a second and slightly larger Shay was on order from the Lima Works, along with $15,000 worth of new ore cars. General Manager Bradford Locke was back in Ohio inspecting the new locomotive, to be named "Russell," and track crews were strengthening bridges and straightening out some trackage.

The "Russell" arrived in Denver on March 5, 1888 and the following day it was brought up to Black Hawk after being transferred to a narrow-gauge flatcar in Golden. She was Lima 199 and weighed twelve tons. Unlike the "Gilpin" the "Russell" had three cylinders and a full cab.

The new locomotive was put into service just in time to start hauling pay dirt from the California Mine on Quartz Hill to the seventy-five-stamp California Mill in Black Hawk. Soon after the trackage to the California was opened, three cars of ore started down off Quartz Hill in the dead of night. The cars derailed on the first switchback; as a former Gilpin Tramway general manager put it, it always seemed that before a runaway the ore was just "run of the mill," and after the crash it was the real "high grade stuff".

On April 6, 1888 Mayor Fick of Black Hawk, accompanied by the marshal, ordered laborers to cease laying a third rail and take up all twenty-four-inch trackage above Selak Street. As has been stated, Mayor Fick was opposed to the tramway and sided heavily with the wagonmasters. Fick opined that the tramway would be detrimental to Black Hawk as it would throw teamsters out of work. "Anything must be done to prevent such a calamity," the short-sighted mayor proclaimed. Nonetheless, the Black Hawk City Council gave Fick the discretion to deal with the Tramway Company.

Fick informed the *Idaho Springs Gazette* on April 14th that "Five four-horse teams and wagons departed this week for Aspen, knocked out by the tramway." Despite the objections of the mayor, the tram tracks stayed after the railway company's clerk informed the local press that the tram intended to pay $450 for the privilege of crossing nine streets and alleys. Black Hawk's City Attorney Livesay informed the mayor that they had better take the money, as there was really nothing they could do to stop an agreement already made between the tram and the Colorado Central. So Mayor Fick backed away from the tram . . . temporarily.

The Gilpin Tramway had won its battle with the teamsters and the mayor. The new railroad cut the mine-to-mill transportation cost from twenty-five to forty-five percent. After the tram arrived, the average cost to move a ton of ore down to North Clear Creek was only 75¢.

The tram owners must have experienced inner satisfaction when the big teaming outfit of Simmons and Clark moved out to Aspen in mid-April of 1888. Others were following suit weekly.

Grading on the line proceeded throughout the spring into Russell Gulch, and on May 23rd six new excursion passenger cars arrived in Black Hawk. The new cars were put into service for a special train of Denver newsmen on June 7th and the papers the following day were full of praise for the little line. The *Denver Republican* remarked: "Passengers standing on the rear platform could hand the engineer a chew of tobacco, should he choose to. Like a hawk in mid-air, the train encircled Central City."

All summer long the tram's foreman, McCormick, and his crew were busy installing stub switches, harp switchstands and sidings to the mine dumps. The total trackage was expanding daily and now totaled over eight miles. Robert A. Campbell had assumed the duties of president of the Gilpin Tramway from Henry Bolsinger, who had many other interests in the district. Bradford Locke was still the chief operating man for the two-foot line.

Excursions were held throughout the sum-

A train of ore drifts downgrade in Chase Gulch, the whistle sounding a warning for any wagons on Smith Road. —John E. Robinson Collection

Excursions were very popular occasions in the early days of the Gilpin Tramway. The first outing was held June 7, 1888 and took Denver newspapermen and their families from the Polar Star Mill in Black Hawk up to tour the California Mine on Quartz Hill. A picnic was held on the return trip, with food provided by Nelson's of Denver. Two photographs of this first of many excursions have survived. At left is the "Gilpin" with a consist of three brand-new excursion cars, while above "Miss Jewett" is photographed in the tiny cab of the Shay. —Henry Hanington, Western Collection, Denver Public Library

mer. An advertisement in the *Register-Call* quoted a round-trip price of 75¢ from Black Hawk and 50¢ from Central, including a picnic lunch. Conductor James Thompson had all the fares he could handle in between bringing down trains of ore to the smelters. Even the *Denver Daily News* offered a round-trip excursion on the "baby railroad" for $2.40 on June 16th, 1888.

Trouble rode in on the morning train from Denver on June 19th. The morning edition of the *Rocky Mountain News* carried a story headlined "An Embarrassed Tramway."

Special To The News from Black Hawk—The Gilpin Tramway was organized about one year ago by R. A. Campbell, B. H. Locke and others to build and operate a two-foot-gauge railroad between this place and Bald Mountain for the purpose of transporting ore . . . estimate made by promoters for construction was $25,000 and upon the representation several Gilpin County men took stock.

Some 8 miles have been made and builders are not able to make an estimate. Some $75,000 to $100,000 has been put in and not yet finished. The rails and most of the material were bought from Union Pacific and the Company issued bonds to pay for them. The amount of these bonds has assumed such enormous figures that the U. P. naturally has assumed control of the Tramway's affairs. Quite a commotion here and indignation engendered, for people were content to have local companies haul ore to keep money invested locally.

Those were fighting words: ". . . the U.P. had naturally assumed control of the Tramway's affairs." Ownership by the Union Pacific was a fate worse than death to many a Western railroad. Before 1886, Jay Gould's tentacles had slithered into the West to strangle private initiative on the mainline rails and on the smaller lines like the Colorado Central. When Charles Francis Adams became president the grip had not been loosened. Now the "Black Hawk correspondent," smelling a great deal like Mayor Fick, had succeeded in "planting" a story that the tram was in the clutches of an octopus.

Gilpin Tramway president Robert Campbell caught the next train for the Queen City and made a personal call upon the editor of the *Rocky Mountain News*. His pleasant manner did not desert him despite his anger. The following day the newspaper printed the following retraction titled "An Error Corrected."

Mr. Robert A. Campbell, president of the Gilpin Tramway Company called at the *News* last evening with a courteous request to correct a misstatement which appeared in the telegraphic columns yesterday.

Your correspondent, said Mr. Campbell "was about as far from the truth as it is possible for him to get. The stock is all held by the original subscribers. The U. P. does not own a single dollar of it. Its bonded indebtedness is $25,000, secured on the whole road, which cost $100,000 and is wholly paid for and held by New England capitalist. The reason the cost exceeded the estimate . . . the road was made longer, the rails heavier, and the general construction more substantial than originally intended. The construction was also satisfactory to the public and to the stockholders." Mr. Campbell's statements are substantiated by several well-known citizens and the correction of a doubtless innocent mistake by a correspondent is cheerfully made.

The director's meeting in Central City in June saw an open quarrel between General Manager Brad Locke and Fred Kruse, the newly appointed secretary-treasurer. The first action the board took was to limit Locke's expenses on his recent trip to Lima, Ohio to $200. Then the matter of Locke's salary arose. Someone proposed that the manager's salary be limited to $100 per month. Locke protested, "Who could live on that?" and reminded the board that he had not been paid in cash since the previous December but had received stock. Locke agreed to accept $400 for the period December, 1887 through June, 1888. Kruse proposed a vote of thanks to the non-salaried officers for their services. He obviously did not intend to include Brad Locke in the thanksgiving, but technically Locke, not having been paid, was a non-salaried officer. Despite motions of thanks all around, the June meeting was not permeated with brotherly love between Locke, the college man with technical training and inherited culture, and Kruse, the self-made man.

Throughout the rest of the summer sightseeing groups rode up to tour the mines in the open excursion cars. Photographer W. C. Steele was kept active making pictures of the various excursions and offering his prints for sale in the Central City Drug Store. The sounds of the Black Hawk Reed and Silver Band provided the background for many of the picnics held above Central City.

New trackage reached above Russell Gulch to the Iron Mine and the Pewabic Mine, and a switchback was constructed to the Saratoga Mine. By the end of August, 1888 the tram was operating fifteen and one-half miles of trackage.

Before the winter of 1888-89 had set in, Brad Locke had completed what he set out to do—put the main mines of Gilpin County on his tram line. Switchbacks were thereafter con-

structed as other mines developed and pulled out as mines slumped, more publicity being given to the building than the pulling. However, Manager Locke had other projects besides laying track. Winter was coming and cold weather presented unusual operating problems for the railroad. Carrying ore in winter is hard, because ore comes out of the ground wet, is loaded into the cars and freezes en route to the mills. Since the custom of the tram was to collect the ore from the mines in the afternoon, leave it at the depot overnight and deliver it to the mills the next morning, the ore had sufficient time to freeze solid. The tramway solved this problem in a very unique and unusual manner. In November, 1888, before the annual Christmas freeze, they built a huge stone warming house.

The warming house was constructed in upper Black Hawk near the engine house. The large stone structure was two-hundred and forty-five feet long, twenty-eight feet wide and seven feet high. Three tracks ran the entire length. Steam pipes running between the tracks, as well as three large stoves, kept the temperature of the interior as high as 120 degrees, even in extreme Colorado cold. The ore of thirty one-cord cars could be dried overnight for delivery the next morning. The warming house was built on a two and a half percent grade so that four cars at a time could be dropped down into the structure by gravity.

Later the huge building was heated by one large boiler instead of three small stoves. Louis Pircher, foreman, remembers that the boiler, which stood in front of the warming house, used large quantities of coal, since it required forty pounds of steam pressure to drive enough steam through the pipes along the walls. During periods of bitter cold, it sometimes took as long as three days to thaw out the cars. Many times they had to pull the cars back from the mills to re-thaw them before they could be dumped.

The winter of 1888 was an unusually bitter one. The mills in Black Hawk shut down in December because the water in North Clear Creek had almost stopped running. The Hubert Mill shut down, although twenty-five miners were still at work at the 600-foot level of the mine.

On Christmas Day, 1888, about thirty of the boys from Central City were playing atop Gunnell Hill. The down train came along, run by an engineer who, in accord with the tradition of the day, was smashed on yuletide cheer. He invited the boys to jump on and see some speed. The kids were wild with glee; they mounted the tender and clung to all available parts of the "Gilpin." The engineer put on all the steam and came down at a pace that delighted the youthful riders but caused obvious concern among their fearful parents. Crowds gathered in the streets of Central as the train circled the town with its load of screaming children. The parents shook their fists at the engineer and cast verbal doubt on his origin.

The belching steamer, with a two-exhaust burst to each rotation of the crankshaft, created an awful sound as it gained speed. The inevitable finally happened—the engine jumped the track and rolled on its side in a gully. By some miracle no one was hurt, but the engineman never touched another Gilpin Tramway throttle. 1888 ended with a bang for the Gilpin Tram.

Gilpin Gold heads toward Golden in the high cars of this Colorado Central train, pictured by stereoptician photographer Alex Martin in Clear Creek Canyon.—State Historical Society of Colorado

At the head of Chase Gulch, the tramway trackage made a sharp curve, crossed the gulch and continued on a five percent grade up Winnebago Hill. Castle Rock is at the left in this 1899 view by Harry Lake, a pioneer Central City photographer. The branch to the Tucker Mill had not yet been constructed.

Gilpin Mines and Miners

It took a hardy breed of men to claw the gold-bearing quartz from the Gilpin mountains. At times they were perhaps prone to hard liquor and soft women when they came down from the mines to live it up in Black Hawk or in Central City. But they were good family men and hard workers, too. Today the huge tailing piles and crumbling shaft houses stand as monuments to their efforts. At left is the mine train of the famous Bobtail Mine in Gregory Gulch. Miners of the Saragota use picks, seven-pound hammers and star drills (bottom left) in this 1889 view. George W. Barret, manager of the Saratoga Mine rides down a vertical shaft on an inspection tour for visiting mining engineer F. W. Endlich in 1889. The Saratoga Mines were a major shipper over the Gilpin Tramway. Everyone had on his "Sunday best" when a photographer made this view (below) of the Grand Central Gold Mining Co., also on a tramway spur. —Western Collection, Denver Public Library

The Black Hawk Reed and Silver Band was usually on hand for such special occasions as an excursion to Excelsior Flat near Russell Gulch. Photographer W. C. Steele was kept active making prints of such outings as this one held on August 30, 1888, attended by six hundred persons. This is the only known photograph in which all six of the Gilpin Tramway Company excursion cars appear. Other excursions were held throughout the summer months. The little railroad's own baseball team, known as the TRAMWAY NINE, would play another local team, and booths would be set up to serve food and Mack's Beer. The public was invited to such outings, and the round trip train ticket up to the flat and back to Black Hawk was only four bits. —W. C. Steele Photographs

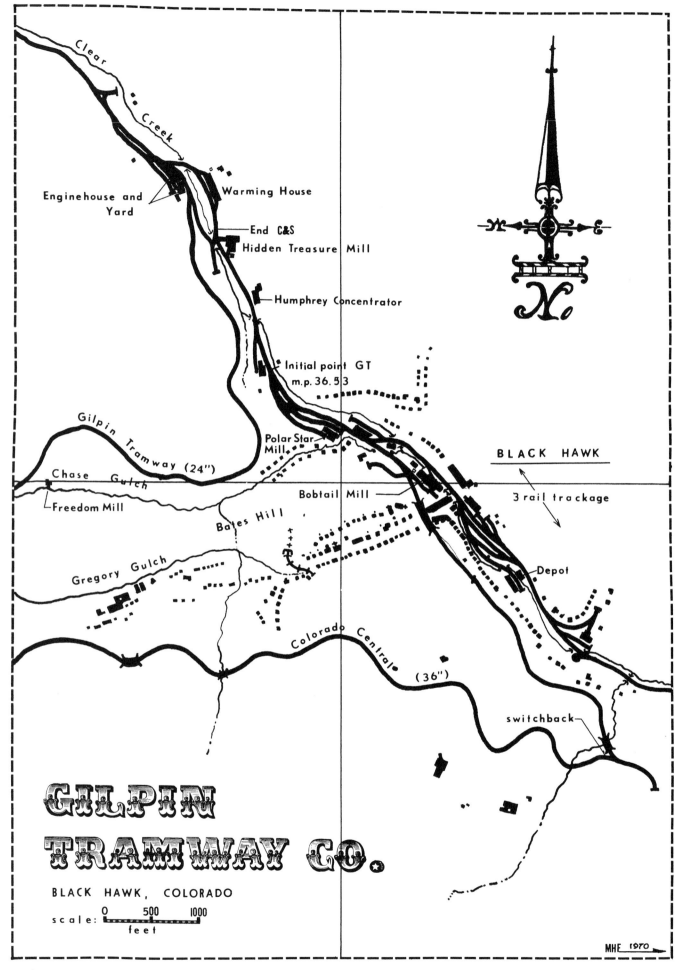

Clear Creek

Enginehouse and Yard

Warming House

End C&S

Hidden Treasure Mill

Humphrey Concentrator

Initial point GT
m.p. 36.53

Gilpin Tramway (24")

Polar Star Mill

Chase Gulch

Freedom Mill

Bates Hill

Bobtail Mill

BLACK HAWK

3 rail trackage

Gregory Gulch

Depot

Colorado Central

(36")

switchback

GILPIN
TRAMWAY CO.

BLACK HAWK, COLORADO

scale: 0   500   1000
feet

MHE 1970

CHAPTER

Running the Tram

January, 1889 saw the Gilpin Tramway Company's board of directors declare a dividend. It was small, one-half of one percent, but notable in that it was the only one ever declared by the little railroad.

Bradford H. Locke's continual problems with other members of the tramway management resulted in his selling $26,000 worth of Gilpin Tram stock to Idaho Springs investors in February. Locke left for Bermuda and England, "to rid himself of a cold," he said.

It took four men to fill Locke's shoes. Frederic Kruse took over as general manager of the line. Thomas A. Potter, president of the Rocky Mountain National Bank, assumed a place on the board; Joseph W. Bostwich became vice president of the tramway; and G. E. McClellan, president of the Idaho Springs Bank, now handled the stock once held by Brad Locke. Bostwich was owner of the Prize Mine, high above Nevadaville; the huge letters are visible on the rusting building to this day.

Brad Locke spent the last years of his life at the exclusive Engineers Club in far-off New York, still a bachelor, and a little pathetic after having been run out of town by irate Cripple Creek miners in 1894. He had tried to increase the working hours from eight to ten hours, and had escaped being killed on the spot by promising never to return to the gold camp.

Frederic Kruse was a native of Holstein, Denmark and had come to Central City in 1860 as a boy of sixteen to join his older brother, Henry, in the grocery business. Young Kruse's trip from the old country was not exactly peaceful, but it probably prepared him for life on the frontier. There was a fire on the ship in mid-Atlantic, an experience which years later must have helped him keep calm as he rescued his daughter from their burning home. He was involved in an Indian attack on the plains, was almost killed on a runaway horse, and was scared half to death by a rattlesnake.

In time, Fred went back east to attend school for two years. The family business prospered, and by the time Kruse took over the tram, he had many interests, including the management of the New York Mill in Black Hawk and serving as an officer of the Rocky Mountain National Bank. He was a great admirer of the theater and especially of Edwin Booth, who apeared at the Central City Opera House. It was this same opera house that was restored in 1931 by Fred's daughter, Ida Kruse McFarlane, and others. It is now a major summer attraction in the historic mining town.

The first thing that Fred Kruse did was to investigate just how much new ore cars would cost the company. He wanted ore cars "with such improvements as experience teaches to be necessary in operating those now in service," he told the Lima Machine Works. In March 1889, twenty new and larger cars were ordered at a cost of $225 each.

The roster of tramway equipment now included twenty three-quarter-ton ore cars, fifty one-cord cars, ten flats and two Shay locomotives. The twenty-one-passenger excursion cars were obviously included among the flatcars.

In the spring, engineers visited the tram to investigate its workings. The mining men in Aspen were considering building a two-foot-gauge railroad of their own up Aspen Mountain to Tourtelotte Park. On March 15th Col. E. E. Pray of Pitkin County was in town to look at the tram as a possible pattern for his proposed Pitkin County Railroad, but little else appears to have been accomplished on this "paper railroad."

Quartz Hill

The most active mining area in the district was known as "The Patch." This group of mines located on Quartz Hill was the largest and longest producer. Their shafts crisscrossed the interior of the hill in every direction, they kept the smelters down in Black Hawk supplied with ore, and the tramway busy carrying Quartz rock down to Clear Creek. The California Mine at one time had the deepest shaft, 2,200 feet, and was often the destination of visiting excursion groups. Here Fred Kruse stands with Shay 3 atop her namesake hill at the California. The smaller view looks across "The Patch" with tramway cars and the Roderick Dow Mine in the foreground. —A. M. Thomas, Western Collection Denver Public Library; H. H. Buckwalter, State Historical Society of Colorado

On May 17, 1889 a spring blizzard hit the tram and no trains were run that day. The "Russell" was sent out with a pilot plow and managed to clear the mainline the following day. The storm made the mill men in Black Hawk happy, as it assured a spring water supply.

After trains were running again, General Manager Kruse left for Lima, Ohio to inspect the new ore cars and place an order for another locomotive.

Spring also saw extension of the Gilpin Tramway mainline. Trackage already had been completed on the short switchback from the Gunnell Dump Shaft to the Grand Army Shaft also on the Gunnell Lode. The mainline contoured Quartz Hill, and the switchback across "The Patch" was being built. The mainline had crossed Leavenworth Gulch en route to the town of Russell Gulch, and former tramway President Henry Bolsinger was fuming because the switchbacks to his Hubert Mine were not being worked on exclusively. He saw Fullerton, of the Grand Army, and Rickard, of the California, shipping ore at reduced rates while he, still a director of the tram, was forced to pay quartz wagon owners to haul his ore.

As the tramway's slim rails were spiked down through Russell Gulch, E. H. Williams began fixing up his store in order to meet the increased business, now that he could bring in goods aboard the tramway trains. By the end of May the railroad extended to the West Frontenac Mine, in which Fred Kruse had an interest.

On June 28th the Gilpin Tramway employees held a picnic in Russell Park. The park was a popular excursion spot near the Missouri Mine with a fine view of the snow-capped range to the west. The public was invited to the employees' picnic, with a round trip from Black Hawk costing 60¢ and from Central City only 50¢.

The new ore cars arrived before the end of June and were soon put into service. There is some indication that the wooden portions of these cars were constructed in the tramway shop, while the metal parts, boxes and trucks were furnished by Lima. It was ten days between the arrival of the cars and the time the first one was placed in service.

On July 12th a much-advertised excursion was held. Several trains were run in order to accommodate the more than one thousand people who came to watch a baseball game between Golden and Black Hawk. The "Russell" was decorated with flags and bunting. The Golden team was delayed because their Colorado Central car jumped the track twice in Clear Creek Canyon. The tramway employees erected a booth for food, but were all sold out by two o'clock. The game, which finally started at three, saw the Golden team win, twenty-seven to nineteen.

Excursions made news throughout the summer of 1889; the Methodists, Knights of Pythias, Episcopals and Old Timers all enjoyed outings on the railroad. But the newspapers also noted that the "Russell" brought down twenty-eight cars of ore on July 26th, and that a double header was necessary a few days later. "Traffic is so heavy," remarked the Central City *Register-Call* "that it keeps the tramway boys rustling these days."

Not to be outdone by the local opera house, the boys of the Hubert Mine converted the shaft building into an art gallery. Naturally, the miner's art was cheesecake, but now the cultural element of Central City had competition. Ten scenes were hung, including "The Flirtation," "The Courting" and two fine chromos. "The boys will add several statues. Now if they will only carpet the floor and secure a dozen or more cuspidors their cup of happiness will be overflowing," remarked an observer.

Section men rebuilt the bridge across Chase Gulch and the upper Eureka Street bridge in September. Heavy cribbing was erected and filled with stone. This work remains intact over eighty years later. Other improvements were made to the right-of-way throughout the summer and fall of 1889, including straightened curves, new fills and wider cuts.

Some mines still used wood for fuel, and the tramway established a wood yard near their Black Hawk shop to store cordwood brought up on the Colorado Central.

On January 3, 1890, Shay 3, the "Quartz Hill," arrived in Black Hawk aboard a three-foot-gauge Union Pacific flatcar. The new locomotive had two trucks, a diamond stack and three cylinders. This was the largest of the little line's engines, and on February 14th she brought down thirty-seven ore cars to Black Hawk. The tram now had ninety ore cars, ten coal cars, some excursion and flatcars, and three locomotives.

The 1890's saw little new construction but continued improvements. An addition was made to the east end of the barn-turned-engine house.

The Shay 2, "Russell," was rebuilt and re-painted early in 1890 and promptly piled up in her namesake gulch. She lay on her side until workmen from the local foundry and the tram-way shop got her back on the rails on March 3rd.

Bad wrecks were infrequent, but local news-papers were full of accounts of a few cars run-ning away or the locomotive jumping the track. Brand-new Shay 3 had her first spill on March 21, 1890—she tipped over while switching at the San Juan Mine high up the switchback on Quartz Hill.

Excursions were still popular during the sum-mer months. The destination was usually Ex-celsior Flat, until recently known as Russell Park. During the season, Excelsior Flat echoed to the sounds of the Gilpin Tram baseball team. Known as the "Tramway Nine," their only re-corded victory was over the Central City Printers team on May 30, 1890. As usual, the Reed and Silver Band was on hand for such outings.

Normal operations saw the tram bring down an ore train using the steam brake on the two-truck Shay, with two brakemen crawling across the loaded seventeen-foot cars to set and release the hand brakes. Despite heavy grades, the Gilpin never saw such refinements as air brakes or automatic couplers. Generally, two trains were run each way every day. Double-headed trains were common when heavy loads of coal and supplies had to be taken up to the mines.

Regular conductor Charles Sneckman and brakeman Zeck Shinner would climb across the rocking little cars to set the brakes on a whistle signal from engineer Sam Doran in the cab. The scream of the flanges against the thirty-five-pound rails was terrific and could be heard for half a mile. The hazards of this job can be ap-preciated more if one considers the problems posed by darkness, a thermometer hovering around zero, and a blizzard blowing snow hard enough to throw a man off balance.

The winter of 1890-91 was a bitter one with high winds piling up drifts in many places. Some days the trains did not make it back to Black Hawk, but the "coasting was splendid on

A Gilpin Tramway train circles Central City on its way up to the mines. Train is on Winne-bago Hill in this photograph made from the Colorado Central grade. —Mallory Hope Ferrell Collection

Shay 3, the "Quartz Hill" carries a group of mining men aboard some new one-cord ore cars in this view near Russell Gulch in the 1890's. —Photograph by H. H. Buckwalter, State Historical Society of Colorado

Moving a Mountain

Gilpin Tramway Shay 3 is shown near Russell Gulch in the two photographs on this page. At left is a very early view in the late 1880's from the collection of John MacNeil. In the mid-1890's the "Quartz Hill" brings down a long train of ore from the Saratoga group in a fine photograph from Richard B. Jackson. The tramway, in its thirty year history moved many a mountain, car by car.

Eureka Hill." The dim glow of the locomotive's kerosene headlight, further dimmed by the blowing snow, combined with the necessity of approaching a drift-covered sharp curve, made a job on the Gilpin Tramway a nightmare for the crew at times. Jack Turney, a veteran engineer, once remarked "I brought her down by braille tonight."

It was not uncommon for a crewman to let a loaded ore car down by gravity. One bitter cold January 17th, Jimmy Tabb, a tramway fireman, was letting down two loaded cars from the Freedom Mine in the dead of night. The sound was heard above the noise of a childrens' birthday party, but no one thought much about it until the next morning when Tabb was found dead in the wreckage at Roundhouse Curve, his hands frozen to the metal brake wheel!

In the middle of the night an ore car jumped the track in the "Dogtown" section of Nevadaville, so noted because of the many prairie dogs that lived there. It was a dark, foggy night and the engine's headlight shone, brightly on a nearby residence, making it appear, from a distance, as though the house were on fire. The Nevadaville firemen were called out of the small frame firehouse, and were highly embarrassed when they arrived on the scene. Ready to do anything to keep the matter quiet, the firemen helped the crew put the car back on the tracks before heading back to town.

May, 1891 saw its usual snowstorm with over a foot of white stuff on the level. With spring came a resurgence of ore shipments over the tram line. On July 31st, the "Quartz Hill" passed Central with thirty-two cars, the largest number noted all summer.

When the Colorado Central became part of the newly formed Union Pacific, Denver & Gulf Railway in 1890, a new agreement was made allowing the continued use of the three-rail trackage from mile post 36.77 to and beyond Black Hawk.

November, 1891 saw an excursion which rated a front page story in *Western Railway* titled "A Two-Footer Railroad."

Twenty-five people, including wives, sisters, and other fellows' sisters, left Denver for excursion on GTC line which is 24 by 20, that is to say, 24 inches wide and 20 miles long. Met by General Manager Kruse who had his private car hooked up to a hot engine . . . began most interesting trip ever taken . . . Climbed up and up for half an hour, could look down on UP tracks that had carried us. As the hawk goes zigzag and at every turn goes higher and higher, so . . . worked their way along rough sides of massive mountains toward the clouds. Our little loco puffed and panted and pulled its way in the direction of the polished peaks of the rugged range . . . just enough danger in trip to make it interesting. At times we trembled on brink of precipice over which we might fall a mile in less than a minute. Where the mountains are too steep, switchbacks are used and in this way a railroad can be built up a tree.

After visiting a number of mines (California) we began descent. Just here we should say a word for the faithful tram crew in whose hands we so cheerfully placed our lives. The young man who let us down the mountain with a steam brake did it as smoothly as has ever been handled down Marshall Pass with automatic air and the smoothest air man in America.

The company owns three locomotives and 120 cars. Trains are run by telephone instead of telegraph. Reach 15 or 20 mines. Daily ore over 400 tons average. Locomotives are of Shay patent and give satisfactory operation. A note of thanks tendered Mr. Kruse at Black Hawk station.

Switchbacks were put in to serve the Leavenworth and Topeka Lodes in the Russell District Other switchbacks were placed to tap the Gold Rock Company's Springdale Mine, the St. Louis-Gunnell Mine, James Henry Mine and Calhoun Lode. The Calhoun Mine buildings still stand high above Russell Gulch. The wind now blows through the tin roof with a creaking sound, but there was a time when the mine was active and the steam boiler was fitted with a number of calliope whistles. Each morning, the men would be called to work as the mine whistles played "Work For The Night Is Coming." In the evening, as the miners left, the whistles played "Home Sweet Home." The miners were not without their social graces in the Gilpin District.

Quartz wagons and Gilpin ore cars were unloaded in Black Hawk at the New York Mill. Note three-rail trackage beneath Shay 3. —Richard B. Jackson collection.

47

As soon as trackage was in at the St. Louis-Gunnell Mine, they began to ship via the Gilpin Tramway, Union Pacific, Denver & Gulf Railway, direct to the Denver smelters. The transfer point, where ore was dumped from the twenty-four-inch-gauge cars into the thirty-six-inch cars, was just above the Polar Star Mill in Black Hawk.

By 1892 many mines and mills were converting from wood to coal fuel. Wood was becoming scarce in the district after thirty years of use as a fuel and for timbering in the mines.

Master Mechanic James V. Thompson was hard-pressed to keep more than a hundred cars and three Shays in operation during the peak summer shipping months. Shay 1, "Gilpin," was used as the Black Hawk switcher, while the heavier "Russell" and "Quartz Hill" handled the mainline and mine work. Many of the earlier ore cars had been completely rebuilt from small one-half and three-quarter-cord cars to full one-cord (ten ton) cars. Jim Thompson later became assistant superintendent of the tram.

Often, extra cars were left atop Gunnell Hill for distribution to the various mines as they were needed. It was found that a number of boys were in the habit of shoving idle tramway cars from the St. Louis-Gunnell spur down a steep grade and piling into the cars for a ride down to the James Henry Mine. The boys controlled the speed with a two-by-four stuck down against the flange. It was a great deal of fun for the boys, but the tramway management was forced to end it in the obvious interest of safety.

Charles P. Tippett, whose father was a miner and also ran the Tippett & Liberman Pool Hall in Central City, recalls that as a lad of twelve he and a neighborhood buddy built their own track speeder out of a pair of discarded mine wheels and used it on the tram until they "got caught."

Water was far from plentiful for the boilers of the many mines. In order to provide water, the Gilpin Tram constructed Water Car 300 from one of the coal cars. The car had a two-thousand two hundred gallon capacity and rolled on twenty-inch wheels. Old waybills give the cost of a carload of water as $10 delivered to the mine. Generally, the water that was pumped from the mines was unsuitable for use in steam boilers due to the high mineral content.

Coal, likewise, was necessary to the operations of the mines, and the tram received $1 per ton for delivering the coal to the mine site. In years to follow, coal would prove to be a motivating factor in the Colorado & Southern purchase of the tramway.

Gilpin Tramway Company trains were dispatched by telephone. In 1892 there were only thirty telephones in the entire district. By asking the operator for "Number seven" you could talk with Master Mechanic Thompson at the engine house. This same number rang the Hidden Treasure Mill, just down the tracks from the engine house. "Number eight" put you in touch with Fred Kruse, the Union Pacific's Black Hawk depot and the tram's president, Robert A. Campbell, in his office at the Public Sampling Works.

Robert Campbell was active in many phases of the civic and mining activities of the area. In addition to being head of the Public Sampling Works in Black Hawk, he was at one time mayor of Central City, superintendent of schools, president of the Athletic Association, and had an interest in a number of mines. While mayor of Central, Campbell shut down all houses of ill fame in the city. This did not win him the popular support of the burly miners, and he was not re-elected in 1895.

When the new gold camp of Cripple Creek became the center of mining attention, Bob Campbell invested heavily in the mines there. It was therefore a great shock on April 29, 1896 when the *Rocky Mountain News* told of a great fire in Cripple Creek and of Robert A. Campbell's suicide. It was a time when financial ruin was striking a number of mining men, for the same paper told of the famous H. A. W. Tabor going into bankruptcy. It was a bad era for those self-made railroad and mining giants who had forged the state. Down in the Silver San Juan Mountains, Otto Mears, the "Pathfinder of the San Juans," had even lost control of his Rio Grande Southern Railroad.

Gilpin Tramway locomotive 3, the "Quartz Hill" poses at the Black Hawk enginehouse with shopmen in this view from the early 1890's.

439
GILPIN TRAMWAY CO.

ENGINEER'S DAILY REPORT.

Black Hawk, _8/15_ 190_4_

The following number of cars were this day hauled by me and entries made at the time of taking them into the train:

Freedom - - -

Grand Central - -

Gunnell - -

Whiting - - -

Grand Army - -

Concrete - - -

Pease Kansas - -

Barnes - - - -

Kansas Burroughs -   *5*

Rome-Gardener - -

Calumet - - - *2*

Old-Town - - - *7*

Avon Mill - - -

Saratoga - - -

Waltham - - -

San Juan - - -

Cyclops   *1*

I hereby certify to the correctness of the above report.

_____
Engineer.

Train No. _____4_____

Above is a Gilpin Tramway engineer's daily report, showing ore cars picked up at the various mines and mills.

Master Mechanic James V. Thompson and his shopmen were often called upon to rebuild bashed-up Shays and repair damaged cars. It was here in the Gilpin Tramway shops, located in upper Black Hawk, that this work was accomplished. When new forgings were needed, the patterns were made and the Eureka Foundry in Central City cast them. In this excellent view we see Shays 1 "Gilpin," 2 "Russell," and 3 "Quartz Hill" lined-up along with the tramway employees in 1890. At far left is General Manager Fred Kruse; James Thompson is sixth from left and engineer Sam Doran is in the cab of the three-spot. —Sam Doran

50

Tram Offices

The Gilpin Tramway used office space located in the Union Pacific, Denver & Gulf stations in Black Hawk (left) and Central City (below).
—Morris W. Abbott; author's collection

The photograph above shows the Colorado & Southern Central City Station in 1920, before the three-foot-gauge was taken up. In the photograph below, taken from the exact same spot in 1949, the station has been completely covered by tailings from the Chain of Mines Mill. The old station lies buried beneath the ore dump. —H. E. High photo; Richard H. Kindig photo.

SHAYS AT HOME

Gilpin Tramway locomotives 3, 1 and 2 line up at the Black Hawk engine house on a sunny day in about 1890. The engine house, which started life as a barn, has been expanded and the warming house can be seen in the background. —A. M. Thomas, Western Collection Denver Public Library. **At left the 3 sports an unusual stack, which obviously did not last too long. The homemade wooden cab indicates that the engine had recently been involved in an accident which removed the original version.** —Edward Bond Collection

Shay 2 brings down thirty-one ore cars past the Freedom Mill in Chase Gulch in 1890. In the photograph (below) a tramway train of coal for the mines heads up-hill on Eureka Street in Central City. —Both photographs W. C. Steele, Western Collection Denver Public Library.

CHAPTER 4
Colorado Road Takes Over

Traffic on the Gilpin Tramway continued to increase throughout the 1890's. The roster continued to grow as new one-cord cars arrived from the Lima Works. The three Shays were kept busy, with the "Gilpin" working the yard trackage in Black Hawk, while the two larger engines worked the mainline.

The two-foot-gauge was not, however, without its problems. On November 29, 1897 Shay 3 jumped the track while double-heading a fifteen-car ore train on the curve just above the Polar Star Mill in Black Hawk. The lead engine rolled down the embankment, demolishing the cab and removing boiler fittings as she went. Engineer Sam Doran, who saw more than his share of tramway wrecks, was slightly bruised. Fireman Will Franklin injured his leg and the three-spot required two weeks in the shop.

As soon as the shop forces had repaired the "Quartz Hill," she was again given to Sam Doran. Coming back down from the Meade Mill on her first trip, she jumped the track again, rolled over and crushed the cab. The crew escaped injury by jumping out of the gangway as soon as the little Shay left the rails.

On Christmas Day, Shay 2 with Dan Williams running her, jumped the track on Prosser Curve and was badly damaged. The engine had been shopped recently and had "stiff universals," which were blamed for the derailment on the sharp curve. The two-spot was so badly damaged that she was sent to the Union Pacific's Denver shops for repairs.

Five days later, on December 30, 1897, the "Quartz Hill" was dispatched on her first scheduled trip out since undergoing extensive repairs. She again left the two-foot rails, but with disastrous results. Sam Doran was again at the throttle of Shay 3 and Will Franklin was back in the left seat. On board that morning was Harvey W. Pierce, who had just been employed as an engineer and was going over the road with Sam in order to familiarize himself with the tram's twisting trackage. As the train was approaching the Eureka Gulch bridge, above Central City, Sam Doran heard an unusual sound and jumped off to inspect the machinery on the right-hand side, walking beside the hard-working engine. Sam had hardly touched the ground when the Shay climbed the sharply curving Prosser Gulch rails and began to tip over on her left side. Before steam could be shut off, the engine rolled off the right-of-way into the gulch. Pierce jumped as the engine went over but was crushed instantly by the boiler. Fireman Will Franklin stayed in the cab and was pulled free by Engineer Doran with the aid of several miners. He was badly scalded, but returned to service after several months of rest in his Black Hawk home.

Shay 3 was so badly damaged that she, too, was sent to the Denver shops of the Union Pacific. This left only the "Gilpin" in operation on the line.

January, 1898 saw the tram unable to handle ore tonnage because of a lack of motive power. Some mines shifted back to ore wagons in order to get their gold ore down to the smelters. In mid-February Shay 3 arrived home and Shay 2 came back to the line in March.

One of the longest trains in Gilpin history was hauled down to the smelters on March 4, 1898, when thirty-six cars came into town behind Shay 3. The train contained a total of two-hundred and eighty-eight tons of ore.

At midnight, January 11, 1899, the Union Pacific, Denver & Gulf ceased to exist and the

The tramway's Shay 3 got into trouble on Prosser Gulch bridge December 30, 1897. A new engineman was killed and the Shay had to be sent to Denver for repairs. —Sam Doran

On December 30, 1897 the "Quartz Hill," fresh from a recent rebuilding after a wreck, was dispatched for the mines with Sam Doran at her throttle and Will Franklin in the left seat. Also on board that day was a new engineer, Harvey W. Pierce, going over the road for the first time. Doran and Franklin were back on the road after recovering from a wreck in which Shay 3 had rolled over and was badly damaged. Sam Doran heard a sound that he did not like, jumped down from the slowly moving engine as she crossed Eureka Gulch and started across the bridge over Prosser Gulch. Then it happened: the three-spot climbed the rails and flipped over into the gulch. Fireman Franklin stayed with the engine and was pulled free by Engineer Doran, but the deadheading engineer was not so lucky. The boiler crushed him as it rolled over and Pierce was dead. Engineer Doran returned later with a camera to obtain pictures of the mess. — Sam Doran, Western Collection, Denver Public Library

Rolling Three Spot

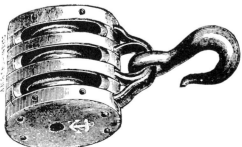

Colorado & Southern Railway took over operation of the vast mountain empire of narrow-gauge trackage built by the Denver South Park & Pacific and Colorado Central lines in the 1870's.

The winter of 1899 is remembered by old-timers as the worst in Rocky Mountain history. In early March the tramway was blocked by a blizzard that dumped huge quantities of snow on the already large accumulation. A special meeting was held of the directors in Central City on March 2, 1899, and it was unanimously agreed to put a large force of men out the following morning in an attempt to clear the tracks of drifted snow.

A number of mines offered their men to help clear the tramway trackage. Early in the morning James Hallihan, the tramway superintendent, had a large army of men out on the right-of-way battling the drifts. The road was opened that day, much to the relief of the mine and smelter men who depended so much on the railroad. Despite the blockage the Kansas-Burroughs Mines on Quartz Hill still shipped four-hundred and twenty-nine cars of ore between March 7th and 28th.

April saw the usual spring snowstorm which tied up the narrow-gauge for several days. Snow shovelers again pushed through deep drifts that blocked the mainline. Spring also saw the tramway extended to the Saratoga Mines east of Russell Gulch and to the Pease-Kansas Mine on Quartz Hill.

At the annual stockholder's meeting on April 29, 1899, with 18,816 shares out of 20,000 outstanding shares represented, it was voted to issue $75,000 in twenty-year, six percent First Mortage Bonds. Some $50,000 worth of the new bonds were already subscribed for and no trouble was expected in disposing of the remainder. All of these bonds were not sold, and it appears that the tram only sold them as it needed money for improvements. The monies received were allocated towards the purchase of a new Shay, new ore cars and track improvements.

Business was so good at the turn of the century that frequently night trains were sent out to Quartz Hill. Nights in the mining district were alive with the sounds of steam whistles, pounding stamps, and honky-tonk pianos.

Locomotive 4 arrived in Black Hawk on February 20, 1900. Slightly larger than Shay 3, she was put to work at once. She was followed two years later by Shay 5, built from the same basic plan.

At the 1902 annual meeting, the Gilpin Tramway Company reported the most prosperous year in its existence. W. L. Bush of Idaho Springs was president, Joseph W. Bostwich of Denver was vice president, while Fred Kruse served as treasurer, secretary and general manager. Directors included the officers plus Lafayette Hanchett of Idaho Springs, R. E. Sloan of Durango and Col. George E. Randolph. Col. Randolph operated the Ophir Mine on Quartz Hill and had been manager of the Denver City Cable Railway Company, which operated cable cars on the Queen City's streets.

The little line never had enjoyed the luxury of a caboose; this situation was rectified in September, 1904 when a caboose was constructed by Gilpin Tramway shopmen. The tiny eight-wheel bobber often graced the end of the tram's daily train until it was destroyed in a runaway.

With the arrival of heavier motive power from the Lima Locomotive & Machine Company, Shays 1 and 2 were sold to an equally two-foot-gauge New Mexico railroad, the Silver City, Pinos Altos & Mongollon Railway. The two Shays were shipped to Silver City, N.M. in August, 1905. These engines retained their numbers on the New Mexico mining road, noted for its loops and curves.

For many years, the mine owners of the region had been plagued by the problem of water seeping into the mine shafts, requiring them to keep pumps going around the clock. The Newhouse Tunnel was to be the answer for mines located on Pewabic Mountain, Quartz Hill and Winnebago Hill. This tunnel, measuring twelve by twelve feet for the first 13,117 feet, was constructed from Clear Creek in Idaho Springs to the very heart of the mining district. The tunnel not only provided drainage for the Gilpin mines, but its underground railroad brought ore out to the Argo Smelter on

The engineer of Shay 4 oils his iron horse during a winter storm. —Mallory Hope Ferrell collection

South Clear Creek. The tunnel was opened in early 1904. It was double-tracked for the first two and a quarter miles and built single track in a nine and a half by six foot tunnel the remainder of the way. The tunnel, while now abandoned, is still considered a major mining achievement, mentioned along with the famous Sutro Tunnel of Nevada's Comstock Lode.

By 1911, the Newhouse Tunnel had reached 4.16 miles under Russell Gulch, Leavenworth Gulch, Illinois Gulch, Nevada Gulch, and Prosser Gulch. It tapped such veins as the Frontenac, Aduddell, King Bee, Saratoga, and the mines of "The Patch," at an average depth of 1,550 feet beneath the surface. Lafayette Hanchett, manager of the Newhouse Tunnel, was also a board member of the Gilpin Tramway Company.

Oldtimers say that it was possible to enter the Bobtail Tunnel in Gregory Gulch and walk underground all the way to Idaho Springs, so complex were the shafts and tunnels of the area. Cave-ins of the past fifty years will prevent the routing from ever being retraced, but it is an interesting story. In later years the Newhouse Tunnel was known as the Argo Tunnel, and the old Argo Smelter still rusts away in Idaho Springs at the southern end of the great tunnel.

Both the Moffat Road and the Colorado & Southern Railroad had long shown an interest

in the tramway as a valuable feeder into their own respective systems. In late February, 1904, Colorado and Southern Vice President J. M. Herbert sent Chief Engineer H. W. Cowan up from Denver to inspect the Gilpin two-foot-gauge. Cowan, after looking over the line and its equipment, recommended that the Colorado and Southern purchase the line in order to prevent it from falling into the hands of "outside parties," an obvious reference to the Moffat Road. The Colorado Road was most interested in seeing to it that the mines of Gilpin continued to use coal from Louisville via the Colorado and Southern, rather than Leyden coal brought in by the Moffat.

Profits of the Gilpin Tramway had averaged a little over $40,000 since 1900 and the Colorado and Southern felt that the little road would be a nice addition to their system. Business on the tram was usually three hundred tons of ore each day, with many new mines near Russell Gulch and Banta Hill requesting extensions of the narrow-gauge. It was decided not to try to convert the tramway to three-foot-gauge because of steep grades (five percent), sharp curves (fifty degrees on some branches) and the close clearances at mine loading bins.

June 27, 1906 saw the Gilpin Tramway Company deeded over to the Colorado and Southern. On July 25, 1906 the Gilpin Railroad

Company was organized by the Colorado & Southern Railroad to take over the operations of the former Gilpin Tramway Company.

Operations of the Gilpin Tramway Company ended at midnight, July 29, 1906, when the line's charter expired. The outstanding funded debt of the tramway consisted of $67,000 in First Mortgage Bonds, which were assumed by the Gilpin Railroad. The entire capital stock of the tram, with the exception of five shares, was pledged to cover the mortgage. The Gilpin Railroad began with an authorized stock of $200,000, made up of 20,000 shares of stock at $10 par value. The line operated as the Gilpin Railroad Company until August 15, 1906, when the name became simply Gilpin Railroad.

Several pieces of rolling stock were added by the new management. A rail car was built to aid in track construction and a much needed four-wheel snowplow was added. Prior to this time, snow drifts had been fought with determination, an army of men with shovels, and wedge plows attached to the front pilot beam of a Shay.

The Gilpin still handled excursion trains after the Colorado & Southern took over; however, all but one of the former excursion cars had been converted for other uses. Generally, coal cars were fitted with crude benches when the tourists came up to ride, and the outings lacked the flavor of the old-time picnics held at Excelsior Flats or Russell Park. In 1908 the Democrats held their National Convention in Denver, and on July 11th, some six-hundred and fifty people rode the tramway and toured the Fifty Gold Mines Mill. The trains consisted of coal cars draped with red, white and blue bunting. Gus Grutzmacher recalls selling rock samples and Columbines, the state flower, to the delegates at the Black Hawk station. After a trip to Pewabic Mountain, the Democrats returned to Denver. Fifty years had passed since the original gold strike in Gregory Gulch.

1910 saw the tramway at its greatest length: 26.46 miles of track, including spurs and sidings. The tram also operated over a little more than half a mile of private trackage above the engine house on North Clear Creek, owned by

R. L. Martin and known as the Fullerton Mill branch.

Unfortunately the Colorado & Southern assumed control of the Gilpin two-footer just at a time when mining was beginning a steady decline that has continued even to this day. Contrary to what many people may think, the gold did not "run out." There is still a great deal of gold-bearing rock in the area, but the cost of processing this ore and getting it out at the deeper levels, combined with the fixed governmental price of gold, has brought an end to gold mining in Gilpin County, the state of Colorado and the West.

Engineer John Tierney with Shay 4 was switching the Aduddell Mine on Banta Hill on March 23, 1912 when the brake beam on Coal Car 11 broke and the car ran away, along with the Gilpin Railroad caboose. Conductor Niccum unloaded from the caboose after tying down the hand brakes. The cars jumped the track and the little caboose was destroyed. The coal car suffered a broken bolster, but no one was injured. It cost $25 to clean up the mess and $393.60 to construct a new caboose in the Colorado & Southern's Denver shop. The second caboose 400 built in October, 1912, was slightly larger. Another caboose was constructed the following year in the Denver car shop. This car, lettered "Gilpin R. R. 401," used trucks from a former excursion car and was delivered in March, 1913.

The winter of 1912-13 was one that Gilpin men remember well. The line was blocked by huge drifts that were reminiscent of the blizzard of 1899. The Irish section boss, Jim Brown, had his men out in the sub-freezing weather in an effort to open the railroad. Billy Goebel, a section hand, recalls that for this bitter nine hours of labor, each of the eight men received $2.02. Drifts exceeded fifteen feet in spots, and the small Shay with its little four-wheel snowplow was often helpless until the men dug out the drifts to a point where the snow train could battle through.

Traffic continued to decline, and by 1914 the railroad was losing $9,750 on its operations. The picture did not improve, and by 1916 only the Polar Star Mill in Black Hawk was treating ores, a far cry from the days when the area boasted sixteen active mills and hundreds of producing mines.

The funded debt on the original Gilpin Tramway Company First Mortage Bonds now amounted to $71,000. Scrap value was estimated at only $48,100 and there seemed very little that could be done except abandon the line. A dispatch was sent out January 12, 1917, ordering all equipment to be brought into Black Hawk by the 15th and the roundhouse locked. The last train operated without fanfare on January 17, 1917.

In February, 1917, Fred N. Rogers appeared at a Black Hawk City Council meeting and requested some tax relief on behalf of the stockholders. However, the historically short-sighted Council rejected this request, thus pulling another spike in the road to abandonment.

The Central City *Weekly Register-Call* carried the following obituary on June 8, 1917:

> Sheriff Mitchell on Saturday last sold all the property of the Gilpin Tramway Company in front of the Court House at Sheriff's sale, the purchasers being M. S. and A. H. Redaskey of Denver. The price offered was $60,000, represented by bonds of the company, which the gentlemen were able to procure at less than thirty-three cents on the dollar. The new owners will scrap the whole of the line with the exception of that portion leading to the Iron City concentrator, from the switch just below the New York Mill, which has been purchased by the mill company, who also bought some 20 ore cars, and ore is being delivered at the mill from cars loaded by wagon in this switch, the cars running down by gravity, and are hauled back by a horse. All the rails, spikes, engines, cars and all other machinery will be shipped to Denver and sold for what it will bring, and the owners are in line for making a good sum of money on their investment.

Otto Blake, who in 1887 had ridden the "Gilpin" on her first trip over the line, was in charge of scrapping the two-foot-gauge. Thus, the thirty year history of Colorado's most unique narrow-gauge came to an end. After the scrapping had been completed, the last Gilpin Railroad engine was loaded on a flatcar, destined for the junkyard. Amos Kearns was at the throttle and Bill Fick was firing. Rails were laid on the top of a flatcar, and the little Shay puffed up with its dying breath. The whistle was tied down, and the death knell sounded into the night.

In early 1898, Shay 1 was hard pressed to keep up with the ore traffic. The line's other two Shays were in the shops for repairs. —Western Collection, Denver Public Library

Big Snow
on the 2 x 20

The winter of 1898-99 was one of the most severe that Rocky Mountain railroads ever battled. January and February saw huge quantities of snow dumped on the 2 x 20, so called because the line was two feet wide and twenty miles long. Early in March another blizzard hit the tramway and operations came to a halt. Mine owners offered their men to help shovel open the tramway's trackage, and the Gilpin Tramway officers held a special meeting on the problem of snow removal. Trackage was finally cleared with an army of men and wedge plows bolted to the front of the Shays. These photographs by Harry Lake show the depth of the snow during the battle to open up the line near the Topeka Mill at the west end of the Quartz Hill branch.

Double headed trains on the Gilpin Tramway were rare occasions and seldom photographed. Engines 2 and 3 blacken the summer sky as they blast up-hill on the Quartz Hill branch with a mixed consist of coal and gold ore in the year 1896. Number 5, the newest and largest of the tram's Shays, poises at Black Hawk in 1902 (above), soon after her arrival on the two-foot-gauge pike.—Author's Collection.

In 1908 the Democrats held their National Convention in Denver and on July 11th, some six-hundred-fifty delegates came up to Black Hawk to ride the tram, now officially known as the Gilpin Railroad. After a tour of the Fifty Gold Mines Mill, they boarded wooden coal cars for a trip to Pewabic Mountain. The cars and engines were draped with red, white and blue bunting. The photograph at the right shows the special train before it left Black Hawk. The little boy in the straw hat, sitting on the derailed original tramway flatcar is Gus Grutzmacher, who recalls selling ore samples and columbines to the visitors. The outing lacked the flavor of the old time trips to Excelsior Flat, but times were changing. It had been fifty years since the original gold strike. —Western Collection, Denver Public Library

No. 3354

DUPLICATE MILL RECEIPT.

Received of Gilpin R. R. Co. Cars Nos.

| 135 | 141 | 49 | 24 |
| 117 | 110 | | |

From _Frazyntenac_ Mine
Date _March 26_ 1962
_Cy_
in charge at _Grant_ Mill.
Train No.

D. W. TAYLOR

Gilpin Tramway Shay 5, with a long train of coal for the mines, passes Winnebago Hill above Central City, shortly after her arrival on the line in 1902. —Harry Lake. **Paper items of the tramway, such as the mill receipt at left, are quite rare.** —Robert W. Richardson collection

Shay 5 is shown with a former excursion car that was rebuilt into a flatcar. —Western Collection, Denver Public Library

Colorado & Southern Superintendent Sol Morse and family took Shay 5 and the remaining excursion car over the road in 1907 for an inspection of the railroad which his carrier had recently purchased. —Louis Pircher.

STORM OF 1913

The winter of 1912-13 was reminiscent of the great blizzard of 1899. Irish section boss, Jim Brown, had his men out in force in the sub-freezing weather in an effort to keep the line open. The Colorado & Southern had to bring their rotary snowplow up to clear the yard-wide trackage, but the tramway had to make do with shovels and their homemade wedge plow. At the top we see Shays 4 and 3 between drifts near Nevadaville, while on the opposite page, Shay 4 battles a deep drift on the tracks across Eureka Gulch (top). This is the only good photograph that shows the tramway's caboose 400, which had been built in October, 1912 to replace the original 400 that was destroyed. Shays 3 and 4 stop for water at the Eureka Street tank on their way back from battling heavy drifts (bottom). —photos by William Ziege

C & S: The Gilpin Connection

COLORADO AND SOUTHERN

The traffic into and out of the Gilpin mining district rode on the twisting Colorado & Southern's three-foot-gauge. The narrow-gauge trackage was built up from Denver in the 1870's and continued to operate as such until the Clear Creek line was finally abandoned in 1941. These two photographs by Richard B. Jackson portray the Colorado & Southern in its final years. Colorado & Southern 70, a 2-8-0, winds the twisting Clear Creek District trackage in the summer of 1940, in a classic photograph of narrow-gauge railroading. At the right, Colorado & Southern 65 takes water at Golden in July, 1938.

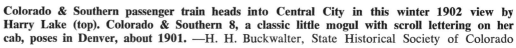

Colorado & Southern passenger train heads into Central City in this winter 1902 view by Harry Lake (top). Colorado & Southern 8, a classic little mogul with scroll lettering on her cab, poses in Denver, about 1901. —H. H. Buckwalter, State Historical Society of Colorado

A Colorado & Southern passenger train pauses at Forks Creek in 1910 (above). It was at Forks Creek that the narrow-gauge line split, one track going to Black Hawk and Central City, while the other continued to Idaho Springs, Georgetown and Silver Plume. —Hungerford Collection. Colorado & Southern 49 heads a Central City bound passenger train in this 1902 photograph by Harry Lake (below). At the left is an interior view of Colorado & Southern combination Car 20, which once brought blackjack dealers, miners and fancy ladies up to the diggings from Denver City. —John W. Maxwell

Gilpin Shay 3 in Black Hawk with crew just before the line quit. The brakemen hold sticks for guiding the links on the link and pin couplers, still used by the two-foot gauge line. Automatic couplers were required on all interstate railroads in 1903, but the Gilpin never got too far from Black Hawk and never interchanged with other lines due to the difference in gauges. —Jon MacNeil collection

This link and pin coupler shows casting marks indicating that it was made by the Colorado & Southern. It was still attached to an ore car at Black Hawk in the 1930's.—Mac Poor

Gilpin Ghost

The countryside surrounding the "richest square mile on earth" is still haunted by the ghost of the Gilpin Tramway and the mines and mills that it served, even more than half a century after the last train ran. It is possible to hike over the major portion of the tramway itself. Beginning in upper Black Hawk, an interesting hike can take you over the first mainline switchback and along the Chase Gulch line in one afternoon. You will see high rock retaining walls placed there in early 1887 by Brad Locke's crews. The old right-of-way eventually crosses over Chase Gulch and winds its way around Winnebago Hill, above Central City and across Eureka Street near the old stone reservoir, site of a tramway water tank. The line can be followed to Nevadaville, population six, which was once larger than Denver. High above Nevadaville, also known as Bald Mountain in the 1860's, the lettering of the old Prize Mine still is visible. Above Central City near the cemetery, the traces of the old wye and numerous branches can be found.

The hike from Russell Gulch past the remains of the Pewabic Mine along the Saratoga and Banta Hill grades will usually reward the Gilpin Tram historian with a tiny spike left in the gold-bearing dirt by the scrappers.

The gulches are virtually littered with the remains of abandoned mines and mills. From almost any point in Central City, the route of the tramway can be traced along the hillsides on three sides of the former gold camp.

In Black Hawk, the remains of the Fifty Gold Mines Mill can be seen behind the service station on State Highway 119. A little further along the north side of the road, the old warming house foundation stands as a tramway tombstone. Here and there are old buildings with nostalgic names such as Polar Star, Frontenac and Bobtail.

The true Gilpin Tram fan may be able to note the wooden beams of several Gilpin Tramway ore cars rusting and rotting beside a small wooden bridge across Clear Creek in Black Hawk. There is still a block of buildings in Central City named after the tramway's president, Robert A. Campbell.

The old Calhoun Mine, that once called the miners to work with a steam calliope whistle, still stands beside the rail-less right-of-way near Russell Gulch.

Photographs of the Gilpin Tramway have long been treasured collector's items. Their rarity was increased by the fact that the railroad ceased operations so long ago. Printed matter from the line has also become a prized item, and until recently none had turned up. Then Robert W. Richardson of the Colorado Railroad Museum discovered a small collection of tramway files among some paperwork discarded by the Colorado & Southern. Deep in the stack of old papers was an original Gilpin Tramway Company stock certificate dated 1889, signed by Robert A. Campbell and Fred Kruse and issued to Bradford Locke, the three most important men in the tram's history.

An old steamer trunk discovered in Central City contained a number of very rare photographs of the tram, which are reproduced in this work for the first time. Every effort was made to gather together all photographs taken of the tramway and to select the best for use in this book.

Yes, the mountainsides are still haunted by many of the wonderful ghosts of Gilpin. The country is as full of historical interest today as it was full of gold when the tram's whistles echoed across the district and the sound of a thousand stamps pounded out history in these hills.

The old Calhoun Mine once called its miners to work with a steam calliope playing "Work for the Night is Coming." The hillsides are alive with Gilpin ghosts. —Mallory Hope Ferrell

In Central City the Colorado Central Narrow Gauge Railroad has been constructed over a portion of the original Colorado Central Rail Road grade between Central and Black Hawk. A beautiful narrow-gauge Baldwin 2-8-0 from El Salvador provides the motive power for this tourist line. Below is a view of Central City today. It is undergoing a revival to the tune of honky-tonk pianos and tourism. —Mallory Hope Ferrell

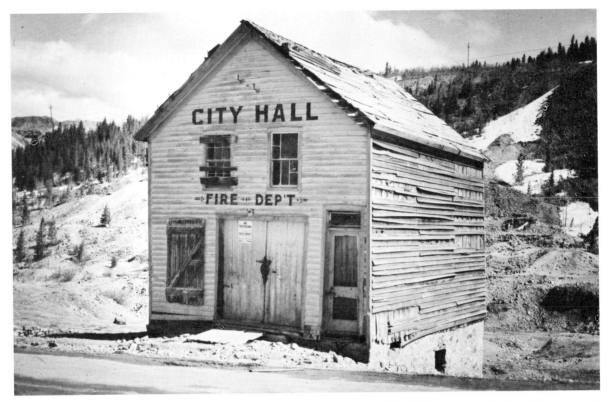

In Nevadaville, once a larger city than Denver, the old Fire House and City Hall still stands. All of the smelters are gone from Black Hawk (below), but the remains of the old Gilpin Tramway transfer can still be seen at the far right. Gregory Gulch, scene of the original gold find, winds its way toward Central City, beyond the hill in the center of the photograph. —Mallory Hope Ferrell

Remains of many mines are still to be found in the area served by the Gilpin Tramway. In Nevadaville (top) the cables of an abandoned aerial tramway hang down in lifeless fashion, while old ore cars lay scattered about. The soil still glitters (left) around the abandoned mines near Russell Gulch. —Mallory Hope Ferrell

END OF THE LINE

The sad task of tearing-up the Gilpin Tramway befell this crew. Otto Blake, who in 1887 had ridden the first train, was in charge of scrapping operations. After abandonment (below) of the tramway, some cars were sold to the Iron City Mill and used on a short, horse-drawn section of former tramway trackage in Black Hawk, until the mill shut down.

Links & Pins

The equipment of the Gilpin Tramway Company was unique and highly functional. The selection of two-foot-gauge trackage was done for economic reasons, but it proved to be a sound choice. Rail was obtained second-hand from the recently standard-gauged Utah & Northern Railway and was of the thirty-five-pound variety.

Locomotives and cars were ordered from the Lima Machine Works of Lima, Ohio or homemade in the line's shop (once a barn for hayburners). Shay locomotives proved very efficient on the steep grades of the road, and the tram purchased five two-truck Shays between 1887 and 1902.

The cars used on the line were of a simple design. The original order for fourteen ore cars was placed before the first rails were laid in 1887. These cars were small, half-cord cars with fourteen-inch wheels. Six more identical cars followed shortly, along with ten small flats and eight coal cars. An order for fifty one-cord ore cars was placed in 1888, followed by an order for twenty more of the same design on May 10, 1889. Eventually, there were one-hundred and thirty-eight ore cars. The original ore cars were rebuilt with higher "boxes" to increase the capacity to three-quarters of a ton. The earlier cars also received new twenty-inch wheels during the rebuilding.

Early excursion photographs show six passenger cars. However, at the time of the Colorado & Southern takeover, only one excursion car remained, and it is apparent that the other five cars were converted into flatcars or coal cars. One such former passenger car appears in a photograph made in the Black Hawk yard. It is the author's opinion that the ten flatcars listed in an 1889 car roster included the six passenger cars.

The line owned eight coal cars, and a water car was constructed in the tramway's shops, as well as a caboose that was built in 1904. When the Colorado & Southern took over operation of the railroad, several new cars were added to the roster. A rail car was built from a former flatcar or coal car, and a four-wheel snowplow was constructed. Under Colorado & Southern ownership, a new caboose was built to replace the Gilpin Tramway Company's original caboose, wrecked in 1912, and another caboose was added the following year.

With the arrival of Shay Locomotive 5 in 1902, the two original Shays were no longer required. So "Gilpin" and "Russell" were sold in August 1905 to the Silver City, Pinos Altos & Mogollon Railroad. They served that New Mexico line until it ceased operating in 1912, then went to a Salt Lake City, Utah copper company and eventually were scrapped.

Gilpin Tramway cars were painted boxcar red with white lettering. They never saw such refinements as automatic couplers or air brakes. The lack of automatic couplers resulted in the nickname "hook and eye line," used by many of the older tramway employees in referring to the entire road. "Hook and eye" was a local name for the link and pin couplers used on the tram and by most narrow-gauge lines in the state until September 1903, when an Interstate Commerce Commission

Any paper item from the Gilpin Tramway is a treasured collector's item. A hike along the abandoned right-of-way may yield a spike or other artifacts from the long-abandoned narrow-gauge. —Mallory Hope Ferrell

GILPIN TRAMWAY ORE CARS

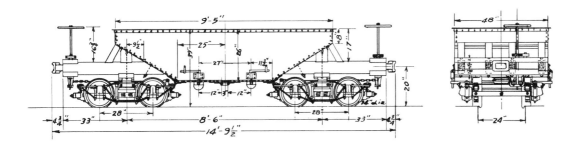

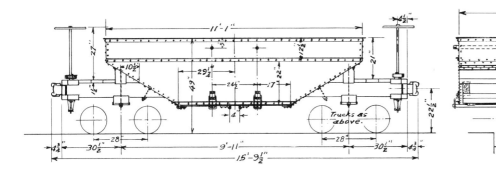

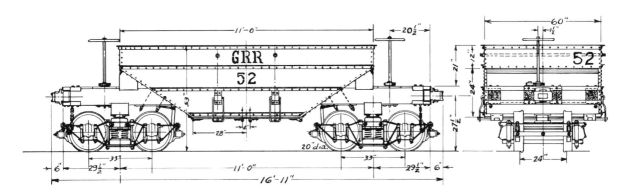

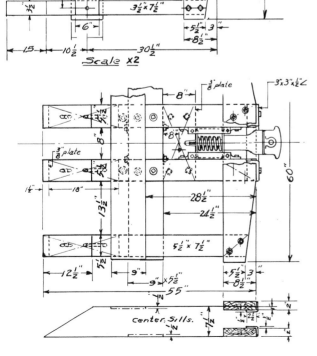

GILPIN ORE CARS
DRAWN BY H. TEMPLE CRITTENDEN

SCALE: 1/4″ = 1′ 0″

The ore cars of the Gilpin Tramway Company and Gilpin Railroad were of a simple design. The first twenty cars of 1887 were small, one-half-cord cars with fourteen-inch wheels. These cars are illustrated in the top drawings. In 1888 an order was placed for fifty cars of one-cord capacity. The second order is illustrated by the center drawings. All of the original cars were eventually rebuilt with twenty-inch wheels and a greater capacity. In 1889 twenty larger cars were ordered and later cars followed the same general design. By 1905 there were 138 ore cars, most of which had been rebuilt to the design shown in the bottom photograph and drawings. —Photographs by Richard B. Jackson

93

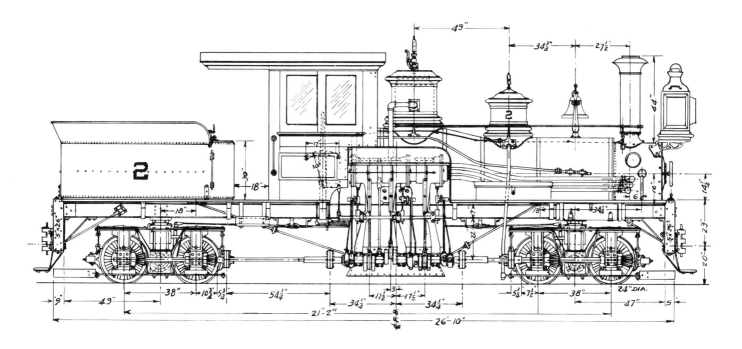

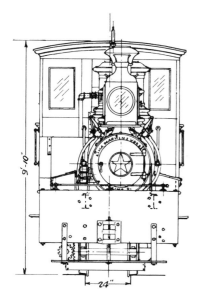

Gilpin Shay 2

GILPIN TRAMWAY SHAY 2 "RUSSELL"
DRAWN BY H. TEMPLE CRITTENDEN
SCALE: 1/4" = 1' 0"
Built by Lima Machine Works, Lima, Ohio.
Construction Number 199
Shipped February 22, 1888
Cylinders: Three 7" x 7"
Wheels: 24" diameter
Weight: 12 tons
Sold August, 1905 to the Silver City, Pinos Altos & Mogollon R.R.

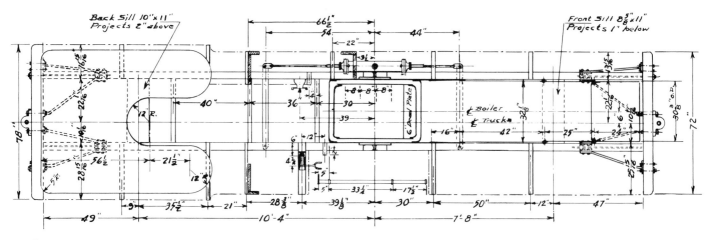

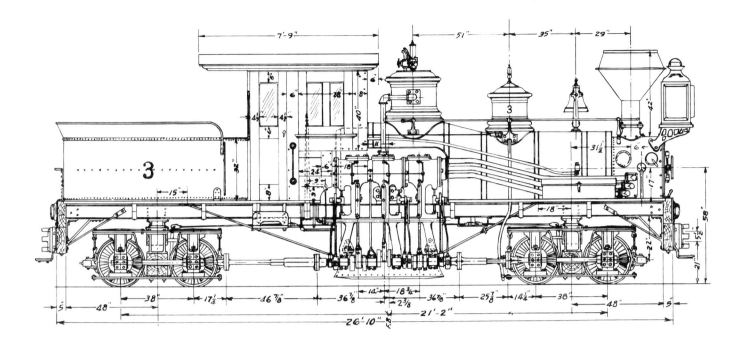

Gilpin Shay 3

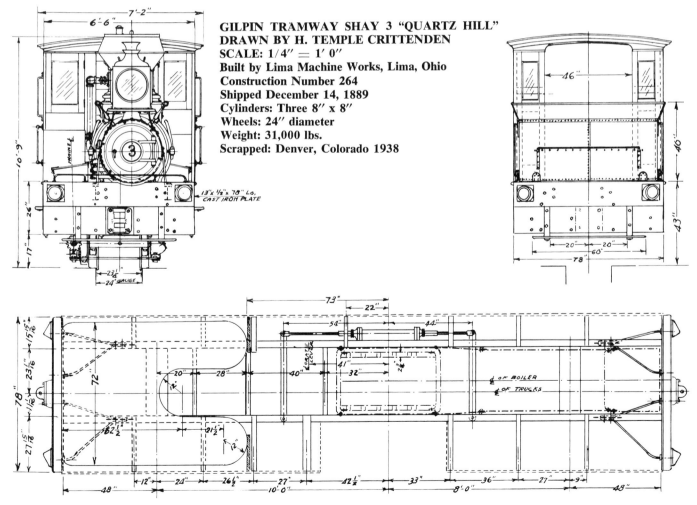

GILPIN TRAMWAY SHAY 3 "QUARTZ HILL"
DRAWN BY H. TEMPLE CRITTENDEN
SCALE: 1/4″ = 1′ 0″
Built by Lima Machine Works, Lima, Ohio
Construction Number 264
Shipped December 14, 1889
Cylinders: Three 8″ x 8″
Wheels: 24″ diameter
Weight: 31,000 lbs.
Scrapped: Denver, Colorado 1938

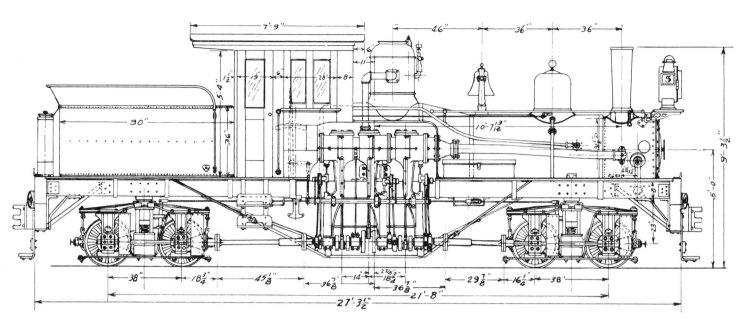

Gilpin Shay 5

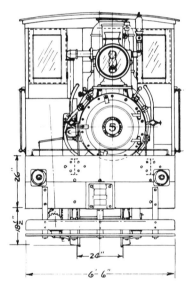

GILPIN TRAMWAY SHAY 5
DRAWN BY H. TEMPLE CRITTENDEN
SCALE: 1/4″ = 1′ 0″
Built by Lima Locomotive and Machine Company, Lima, Ohio
Construction Number 696
Shipped April 23, 1902
Cylinders: Three 8″ x 8″
Wheels: 24″ diameter
Weight: 36,200 lbs.
Scrapped: Denver, Colorado, 1938

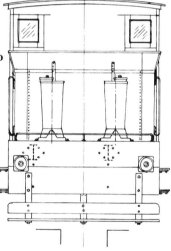

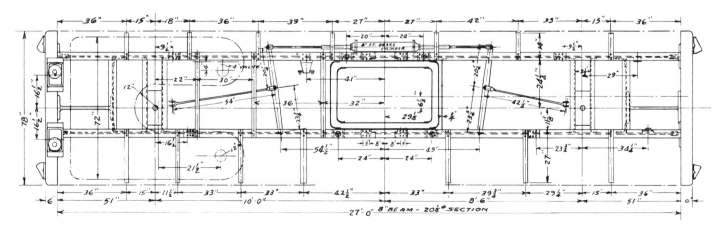

G. T. Caboose

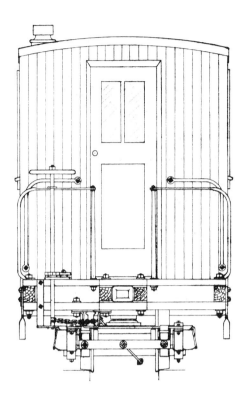

GILPIN RAILROAD CABOOSE 400
DRAWN BY JOHN E. ROBINSON
SCALE: 3/8″ = 1′ 0″
Built by Colorado & Southern Shops
Date Built: October, 1912
Length: 14′ - 2″   Body 10′ - 6″
Width: 6′ - 0″
Replaced original Gilpin Tramway Caboose 400, destroyed March 1912

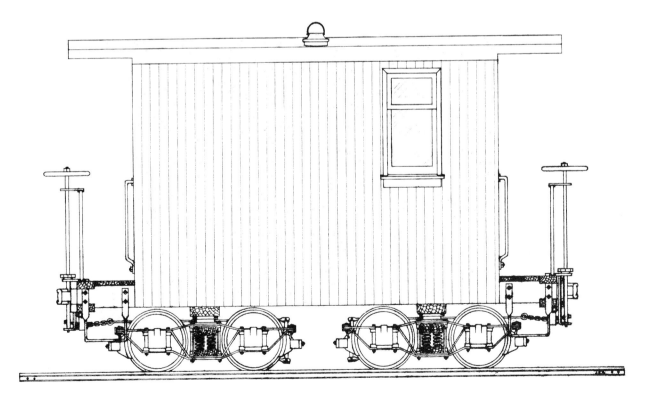

law required automatic couplers on all equipment used for interchange or interstate travel. Since the tramway never interchanged because of its gauge, and it never got outside the "Little Kingdom of Gilpin," the management never converted from the use of the link and pin coupler.

Steam brakes were fitted to the Shay locomotives, but brakemen with clubs had to climb across the loads to apply and release brakes on the cars.

When the Gilpin Railroad was abandoned in 1917, twenty steel ore cars were sold to the Iron City Mill. They were used on a horse-drawn section of the former tramway trackage between a loading point just below the New York Mill and the Iron City concentrator. The cars were loaded and dropped down to the concentrator by gravity. After unloading, they would be hauled back upgrade by horse power. This operation was continued until about 1930. As late as 1970, some parts of the cars were still to be seen in lower Black Hawk.

Other Gilpin cars were offered for sale by Denver's Morse Brothers Machinery Company, and Shays 3, 4 and 5 were converted to three-foot-gauge in the hope of finding a buyer. All three engines were eventually scrapped in 1938 after rusting away for twenty years.

Shay 4 is shown in Denver's Morse Brothers scrap yard before it was scrapped in 1938. Gilpin engines 3, 4 and 5 were converted to three-foot-gauge, in hopes of selling them, but a buyer never came. —Richard H. Kindig collection

SHAYS GO SOUTH

Gilpin Tramway Shays 1 and 2 were sold in August 1905 to the two-foot gauge Silver City, Pinos Altos & Mogollon Railroad of Silver City, N. M. This mining line extended a distance of eight miles from Silver City to Pinos Altos, using sharp curves and a loop (above). —H. Temple Crittenden. **Gilpin's former Shay 1 is shown (right) on the first excursion over the new railroad on January 1, 1906, at the Farnsworth Ranch, three miles north of Silver City. —Nelson Gray from David Rees Collection. When the New Mexico two-footer finally folded, former Gilpin Shay 2 was loaded aboard a flatcar and sent to Salt Lake City copper company (below) in 1913.**

G. T. Cars

GILPIN TRAMWAY - CAR ROSTER

The roster which follows was discovered among some aging Colorado & Southern paperwork in 1969. It is a listing of equipment dated 1915 and has notations from earlier rosters in existence (1889, 1908, 1910), and information taken from old letters and photographs.

Number	Type	Length	Width	Cap.	Cost (C&S)	Remarks
01	Rail & Boiler	21′ 0″	5′ 0″	15,000#	$200	Built by C&S 1906. 20″ wheels.
02	Snow-plow	13′ 6″	4′ 8″	—	$150	Built by C&S 1906. 20″ wheels.
1-3	Flat	17′ 0″	3′ 8″	8,000#	$ 50	Original cars of 1888. 14″ wheels. No. 3 converted to coal car No. 14.
4	Flat	21′ 0″	5′ 0″	20,000#	$200	Former excursion passenger car. Rebuilt to large flatcar.
5	Coal	17′ 0″	3′ 0″	8,000#	—	Original car, never rebuilt. 14″ wheels. Last appeared on June 1910 roster. Original flat.
6-13	Coal	21′ 0″	5′ 0″	20,000#	$250	Original 8 wooden coal cars. 20″ wheels. No. 13 off roster before March 1915.
14-17	Coal	— See Remarks —				Car No. 14 converted from flatcar No. 3. After 1908 no cars No. 15, 16, 17 listed. Probably used for parts.
18-37	Ore	17′ 7″	5′ 0″	13,200#	$325	Original half-cord cars of 1887, rebuilt to three-quarter-cord capacity with 20″ wheels in place of original 14″ wheels. Car No. 34 destroyed March 1914.
38-87	Ore	17′ 7″	5′ 0″	20,000#	$250	Order of 50 one-cord cars of 1888. Car No. 85 destroyed March 1914.
88-155	Ore	17′ 7″	5′ 0″	20,000#	$325	20 one-cord cars ordered May 10, 1889.
300	Water	23′ 0″	5′ 0″	20,000#	$500	Built by GTC. Capacity 2,200 gallon. Cost to mine for this car of water was $10.
400-1st	Caboose	13′ 2″	6′ 0″	—	—	Built by GTC, September 1904. Originally had 14″ wheels, converted to 20″ wheels. Destroyed March 23, 1912.
400-2nd	Caboose	14′ 2″	6′ 0″	—	$393	Built by C&S Denver shops, October 1912.
401	Caboose	14′ 2″	6′ 0″	—	$316	Built by C&S Denver shops, March 1913. Trucks from excursion car.
500	Excursion	21′ 0″	5′ 0″	21 passengers	$200	There were originally six excursion cars in 1888. No. 500 is only car to survive until C&S ownership. Other passenger cars converted to other uses. One appears to have been converted to a rail & boiler car in 1906. Another passenger car bacame flat No. 4. Car No. 500 renumbered observation car No. 1 in 1915, as flatcar No. 1 was out of service by that time.

Locomotive Roster

SHAY LOCOMOTIVES OF THE GILPIN TRAMWAY COMPANY
Two-foot-gauge, two-truck Shays, purchased new

Road Number	Builder	Date	Number	Cylinders	Wheels	Weight	Remarks
1	Lima	Aug. 10, 1887	181	2 - 7″ x 7″	24″	20,000#	Sold August 1905 to SCPA&M, Silver City, N.M. To: Savannah Copper Company, Salt Lake City, Utah in 1913 for storage. Scrapped prior to WWI.
2	Lima	Feb. 22, 1888	199	3 - 7″ x 7″	24″	24,000#	Same as No. 1.
3	Lima	Dec. 14, 1889	264	3 - 8″ x 8″	24″	31,000#	To: M. S. and A. H. Redaskey, Denver. Converted to 36-inch-gauge for possible sale. Scrapped 1938.
4	Lima	Jan. 27, 1900	594	3 - 8″ x 8″	24″	34,800#	Same as No. 3.
5	Lima	Apr. 23, 1902	696	3 - 8″ x 8″	24″	36,200#	Same as No. 3.

Mines Served by the Gilpin Tram

MAJOR MINES SERVED BY THE GILPIN TRAMWAY

Aduddell
Anchor
Avon
Ayres Leavenworth
Banta Hill
Barnes
Belden
Buckey
California
Calhoun
Castle Rock
Charter Oak
Climax
Concrete
Danby
East Pewabic
English Morros
First National
Fourth of July
Freedom
Frontenac
Gardner
Gettysburg
Grand Army
Grand Central
Gunnell
Hawley
Hazeltine

Hubert
Kansas Burroughs of Phoenix Burroughs
Lotus
Macky Burroughs
Old Town
Ophir Burroughs
Pease
Pease-Kansas
Pocahontas
Prize
Protection Shaft
Queen Bee
Queen of the West
Reed Leavenworth
Robert Emmet
Roderick Dow
San Juan
Saratoga No. 1, No. 2, No. 3
Stroub
Topeka
Tucker
Twoton
Walhala
Waltham
Whiting
Woods
Woutouge

—William Ziege

MILLS SERVED BY THE GILPIN TRAMWAY
1888 - 1917

Arrighi and White
Avon
Becker
Bobtail
Brooklyn
Burro
Cashier
Empire
Freedom
Fullerton
Gregory-Bobtail
Hidden Treasure
Humphrey Concentrator
Iron City
Meade
Mides
Missouri
New York
Polar Star
Randolph
Topeka
Tucker
Wheeler and Sullivan (later Wheeler)

GULCHES CROSSED BY THE GILPIN TRAMWAY

Chase
Davenport
Eureka
Fourmile
Gregory
Illinois
Leavenworth
Nevada
Packard
Prosser
Russell
Spring
Willis

—Luella Fritz

Albro, Capt. Oliver M.
  Director of 1872 Gilpin Tram.
Bates, John
  Fireman—tore off big toe in August, 1888.
Beebe, Walter
  Sprained ankle jumping from tramway train, December, 1897.
Brill, Joe
  Fireman and later engineer.
Boellert, Mack
  Owner of quartz wagons, purchased stock in Gilpin Tram.
Bogart, W. E.
  Roadmaster for Colorado & Southern.
Bolsinger, Henry C.
  First Gilpin Tramway president.
  Member of GTC board of directors.
  Owner of Hubert Mine.
  Colorado State Senator.
Bostwich, Joseph W.
  Gilpin Tramway vice-president, stockholder.
  Owner of the Prize Mine.
Broderick, Dick
  Section hand.
Brown, Jim
  Section boss.
Bush, W. L.
  Tramway president in 1902.

Campbell, Robert A.
  Director of GTC, 1886.
  Secretary of GTC, 1886.
  President of GTC, 1887.
  Mining man.
Cowan, H. W.
  Surveying engineer for Colorado & Southern.
  Inspected GTC, 1895-96, 1904.
  Submitted report which resulted in the purchase of the GTC by C & S.
Dines, O. L.
  President of Gilpin RR, 1906.
Doran, Sam
  Longtime GTC engineer.
Fick, William
  Mayor of Black Hawk who opposed tramway.
  Black Hawk blacksmith.
Fleckenstein, Andy
  Section boss and later superintendent of the tram.
Franklin, Will
  Fireman.
Fullerton, William
  Mine and mill owner.
Goebel, Billy
  Section hand.
Gorsline, William R.
  Attorney for 1872 tramway.

Bibliography

BOOKS

Fleming, Howard, *Narrow Gauge Railways In America,* Oakland: Grahame Hardy, 1949

Hall, Frank, *History of Colorado,* Chicago: Blakely Printing Co., 1891

Hollenback, Frank R., *The Gilpin Tram,* Denver: Sage Books, 1958

Kindig, R. H.; Haley, E. J.; Poor, M. C., *Pictorial Supplement to DSP&P,* Denver: World Press, Inc., 1959

Shaw, Frederic, *Little Railways of the World,* Berkley: Howell-North, 1958

Ranger, Dan, *Pacific Coast Shay,* San Marino: Golden West Books, 1964

Beebe, Lucius; Clegg, Charles, *Narrow Gauge In The Rockies,* Berkeley: Howell-North, 1958

Poor, Henry V., *Poor's Manual,* New York: H. V. and H. W. Poor, 1880, 1889, 1890, 1891, 1895, 1899

PERIODICALS

Crittenden, Henry T., "The Gilpin Railroad", *Railway & Locomotive Historical Society, Inc., Bulletin 57,* January 1942, pp. 94-98

"The Shay Locomotive", *Engineering News,* XXXII, April, 1890, pp. 386-387

Arps, Louisa Ward, "The Gravity Tram of Gilpin County", *Brand Book 1968,* The Denver Westerners, Inc., Johnson Publishing Co.

NEWSPAPERS

Complete files of the following newspapers:

Register-Call, Central City, Colorado

Boulder Daily Camera, Boulder, Colorado

Daily News, Denver, Colorado

Denver Times, Denver, Colorado

Rocky Mountain News, Denver, Colorado

Railroad Gazette, New York, New York

Index

Accidents
  Aduddell Mine, 64
  Black Hawk, 24
  California Mine, 24-25
  Christmas Day, 30
  Doran, Sam, 59
  Franklin, Will, 59
  Hidden Treasure Mill, 24
  Meade Mill, 24, 59
  Nevadaville, 45
  Polar Star Mill, 24
  Prosser Gulch, *58, 59, 60-61*
  Quartz Hill, 24, 41
  Roundhouse Curve, 45
Adams, Charles Francis, 28
Aduddell Mine, 64
Aduddell vein, 63
Apex, 10
Argo Smelter, 62, 63
Argo Tunnel, 62-63
Aspen, 25, 37

Bald Mountain, 28. *See also*
  Nevadaville
Baldwin 2-8-0 locomotive, *86*
Banta Hill, 63
Banta Hill grade, 85
Barret, George W., *33*
Bates Lode, 9
Beebe, Walter, 24
Black Hawk, *10, 16, 87*
  charter, 10
  map, *36*
  opposition to Gilpin Tramway,
    22, 24
  source of name, 11
Black Hawk City Council, 25
Black Hawk Reed and Silver Band,
  29, *34*, 41
Blackhawk Mining Company, 11
Blake, Otto, 65, *89*
Bobtail building, 85
Bobtail Mill, 22
Bobtail Mine, mine train, *32*

Bobtail Tunnel, 63
Boiler car, 100
Bolsinger, Henry C., 19, 25, 40
Booth, Edwin, 37
Bostwich, Joseph W., 37, 62, 106
Brakes, 98
Brown, Jim, 64, 76
Burlington & Missouri River
  railroad, 106
Burroughs Lode, 9
Bush, W. L., 62

Caboose 400, 77
  built, 64
  design, *97*
Caboose 401
  built, 64
Calhoun Lode, 45
Calhoun Mine, 45, *84, 85*
California Mill, 24
California Mine, 24-25, 27, *38-39,*
  40
Campbell, Robert A. (Bob), 19,
  25, 28, 85
  buildings in Central City named
    after, 85
  civic and mining activities, 48
  correction of *Rocky Mountain
    News* story, 28-29
  Gilpin, James Peak & Middle
    Park Railway, 106
  suicide, 48
Casey [teamster], 11
Castle Rock, *31*
Castro Lode, 9
Central City, *10, 16, 41, 53, 56,
  80, 86*
  charter, 10
  Drug Store, 29
  fire, 10, 12
  Opera House, 37
Central City *Daily Register*, 12
Central City Printers baseball team,
  41

Central City *Register-Call*, 28, 40
Central City *Weekly Register-Call*,
  65
Chain of Mines Mill, 53
Chase Gulch, *20, 25, 31*
  bridge, 40
  Tramway construction, 21
  wagon road, 11
Cheyenne, 11
Clear Creek, 9, 11, 62. *See also*
  North Clear Creek, Gregory
  Gulch
Clear Creek Canyon, *15, 30*
Coal, 48, *56*, 63
Colorado & Clear Creek Railroad,
  11. *See also* Colorado Central
  Rail Road Company
Colorado & Southern Railroad
  Central City Station, *53*
  combination Car, 20, *81*
  locomotives, *78-79, 80, 81*
  passenger train, *80, 81*
  takeover of Tramway, 48, 63-64
  takeover of Union Pacific
    mountain trackage, 62
Colorado Central Narrow Gauge
  Railroad, 86
Colorado Central Rail Road
  Company (*see also* Union
  Pacific, Denver & Gulf Railway)
  and Colorado & Clear Creek, 11
  and Colorado and Southern, 62
  and Gilpin Tramway, 22
  and Union Pacific, 28
  Black Hawk lines, 11-12, 19, 22
  boxcar, *16*
  excursion train, *17*
  flatcars, 11
  gauge for mountain lines, 11
  gold train, *30*
  Golden roundhouse, *14*
  lines from Golden, 11
  locomotives, 11, *14-17*
  mining machinery transport, *17*

passenger train, *17*
Colorado Railroad Museum, 85
Colorado Railway, 106
Couplers, 82, 91-98
Cowan, H. W., 63
Cripple Creek fire, 48

Daily Register (Central City), 12
Darcey, Mr., 12
Dean Lode, 9
Democratic National Convention, 64
    excursion, *70-71*
Denver & Rio Grande Railway, 11, 19
Denver & Salt Lake railroad, 106
Denver & Western railroad, 106
Denver City Cable Railway Company, 62
Denver Daily News, 28
Denver, Northwestern & Pacific Railroad, 106
Denver Pacific Railway, 11
Denver Republican, 25
Denver South Park & Pacific railroad, 62
Denver, Utah & Pacific Railroad, 106
Derailments. *See* Accidents
Dispatching of trains, 48
Doran, Sam, 41, 50-51, 59, 60
Double-headed train, *68-69*

Elk Meadow, *14*
Endlich, F. W., *33*
Eureka Foundry, 24, 50
Eureka Street, 22
    bridge, 40
    water tank, *77*
Excelsior Flat, *34-35*, 40, 41

Farnsworth Ranch, 99
Fick, Mayor William (Bill), 28, 65
    opposition to Gilpin Tramway, 22, 24
Fifty Gold Mines Mill, 64, 70, 85
Fleming, Howard, 19
Forks Creek, 81
Franklin, Will, 59, 60
Freedom Mill, 21, *56*
Freedom Mine, 45
Frontenac building, 85
Frontenac vein, 63
Fuel for mines and mills, 48
Fullerton Mill branch, 64
Fullerton, William, 19, 22, 24, 40

Fullerton stamp mill, 22

Georgetown, 81
Gilpin & Clear Creek District Railway, 106
Gilpin County, 10-11, 64-65
Gilpin County Tram Railway Company, 12
Gilpin, James Peak & Middle Park Railway, 106
"Gilpin" locomotive. *See* Shay 1 locomotive
Gilpin Railroad, 63-65. *See also* Gilpin Tramway Company
    mill receipt, *72*
Gilpin Tramway Company (*see also* Gilpin Tramway operations)
    agreement with Colorado Central, 22
    agreement with Union Pacific, Denver & Gulf Railway, 45
    alleged financial dependence on Union Pacific, 28
    annual meeting, 62
    baseball team, 34
    capitalization, 19
    competition with teamsters, 22, 25
    deeded to Colorado and Southern, 63-64
    directors, 62
    directors' meeting, 29, 62
    dividend, 37
    end of operations, 64
    engine house, 21
    engineer's daily report, *50*
    files, 85
    financial backing, 28-29, 62
    Gilpin Railroad company, 63-65, *72*
    map, *36*
    officers, 25, 37, 62
    offices, 21, *52*
    organization, 19
    paperwork, *90*
    persons connected with, 104-105
    profits, 63
    quarrel between Locke and Kruse, 29
    right-of-way, 22, 25, 40, 85
    stock certificate, *18*
    stockholder's meeting, 62
Gilpin Tramway operations (*see also* Gilpin Tramway Company)
    accidents. *See* Accidents
    cabooses (*see also* Caboose 400,

Caboose 401)
    construction, 62, 91
    roster, 100
cars (*see also* Gilpin Tramway operations, ore cars, etc.)
    coupling, 91-98
    paint, 91
    roster, 100
circling Central City, *41*
coal cars
    converted excursion cars, 91
    number, 91
    roster, 100
    use on excursion train, *70-71*
construction, 21-22, 24, 28
construction crew, *20*
construction train, *23*
derailments. *See* Accidents
employee picnic, 40
end of operations, 65
engine house, 21, *23*, 48, *54-55*
    addition, 41
equipment, 21, 37, 41, 48
excursion cars, 25, *34-35, 75*
    converted to other uses, 64
    number of, 91
    rebuilt into flatcar, *74*
    roster, 100
excursion trains, 64
excursions, 22, 25-29, *26-27, 34-35*, 40, 41, 45, 64
fare, 28, 34, 40
first rails in place, 19, 21
first ore shipment, 22-24
flatcars
    converted excursion cars, 91
    number, 91
    rebuilt from excursion car, *74*
    roster, 100
grading, 21, 25
locomotives. *See* Shays 1, 2, 3, 4 and 5
night trains run, 62
normal operations, 24, 41
ore cars, 21, *42-43*, 85, *88, 89*
    capacity, 48
    cost, 37
    design and construction, 40, 91, *92-93*
    number, 91
    ordered, 24, 59
    roster, 100
    run by gravity, 45
    sold, 65, 98
    used for excursion, 22
ore tonnage, 40, 63

ore train, *25*
passenger cars. *See* Gilpin Tramway operations, excursion cars
pattern for other railroads, 37
private trackage, 64
rail cars, 64, 91, 100
runaway cars, 24
scrapped, *89*
shops, 21, 50, 91
smelter, 11
spur, 33
switchbacks, 24, 29
   Gunnell Dump Shaft to Grand Army Shaft, 40
   Hubert Mine, 40
   list, 45
   Meade Mill, 24
   "The Patch," 40
telephones, 48
trackage, 25, 29, *31*, 40, 64
traffic, 59
transportation costs, 25
trestle, *23, 24*
warming house, 29, *54-55*, 85
water car, 48, 91, 100
water tank, 77, 85
Western Railway account, 45
wood yard, 40
wrecks. *See* Accidents
Goebel, Billy, 64
Gold Rock Company, 45
Golden
   railroad lines, 11
   roundhouse, *14*
Gould, Jay, 11, 28
Grand Army Shaft, 24, 40
Grand Central Gold Mining Company, *33*
Gregory Gulch, 9-11, 63. *See also* Clear Creek
Gregory, John H., 9
Gregory Lode, 9
Gregory Mill, 22
Grutzmacher, Gus, 64, *70-71*
Gulches crossed by Tramway, 103
Gunnell Dump Shaft, 40
Gunnell Hill, 30
Gunnell Lode, 9, 40
Gunnell Mine, 19

Hallihan, James, 62
Hanchett, Lafayette, 62, 63
Hawley, Henry J., 19
Herbert, J. M., 63
Hidden Treasure Mill, 22, 24, 48
Hill, Professor Nathaniel P., 10,

11
"Hook and eye line," 91
Hubert Mill, 29
Hubert Mine, 19, 40
Humphrey's Concentration Works, 21

Idaho Springs, 81
Idaho Springs Gazette, 25
Idaho Springs investors, 37
Illinois Gulch, 24, 63
Interstate Commerce Commission, 91-98
Iron City Mill, 89, 98
Iron Mine, 29
Isabella Mine, 19

James Henry Mine, 45, 48
"Jewett, Miss," *27*
Josephine Mine, 19

Kansas-Burroughs Mines, 62
Kansas Lode, 9
Kansas Pacific railroad, 11
Kearns, Amos, 65
King Bee vein, 63
Kruse, Frederic, *38-39*, 48, *50-51*, 85
   biographical information, 37
   general manager of Tramway, 40, 45, 62
   Gilpin, James Peak & Middle Park Railway, 106
   quarrel with Locke, 29
   secretary/treasurer of Tramway, 62
   West Frontenac Mine, 40

Lake, Harry, 31
Leahy, Edmond, 12
Leavenworth Gulch, 40, 63
Leavenworth Lode, 45
Leyden, 63
Lima Locomotive & Machine Works, 91
   one-cord cars, 59
   ore cars, 21, 37
   second Shay ordered, 24
Lima 199. *See* Shay 2 locomotive
Livesay [Black Hawk City Attorney], 25
Locke, Bradford H., 21, 25, 28, 85
   builder and manager of Tram, 19
   construction techniques, 22
   inspection of new locomotive, 24
   later life, 37

quarrel with Kruse, 29
salary and expenses, 29
sale of Tramway stock, 37
Slaughter House case, 19
Locomotives (*See also* Baldwin 2-8-0, Colorado & Southern, Colorado Central, Porter Bell 0-4-0 tender, Shays 1, 2, 3, 4 and 5)
   roster, 101
   Shay-geared, 21
   source, 91
Louisville, 63
Loveland, W. A. H., 11

Mack's Beer, 34
Mack's Brewery, 19
Martin, Alex, 30
Martin, R. L., 64
Mammoth Gulch, 12
McClellan, G. E., 37
McCormick [foreman], 25
McFarlane, Ida Kruse, 37
Meade Mill, 24
Mears, Otto, 48
Michigan Valley, 12
Mill receipt, *72*
Miller, George, 24
Mills served by Gilpin Tramway, 103
Mines served by Gilpin Tramway, listing, 102
Missouri Mine, 40
Mitchell, Sheriff, 65
Moffat, David, 106
Moffat Road, 63
Montana Diggins, 9
Morse Brothers Machinery Company, 98
Morse, Sol, 75
Mountain City Trestle, *15*

Narrow Gauge Railways in America, 19
Nelson's of Denver, 27
Nevada Gulch, 63
Nevadaville
   abandoned aerial tramway, *88*
   Fire house and City Hall, *87*
   population, 85
New York Mill, 37, *46-47*, 65, 98
Newhouse Tunnel, 62-63
Niccum [Conductor], 64
North Clear Creek, 11, 12, 25

Ophir Mine, 62

Pactolus Road, 106
Palmer, General William Jackson, 11
"Patch, The," *38-39*, 40, 63
Pease-Kansas Mine, 62
Pewabic Mine, 29, 85
Pewabic Mountain, 62, 64, 70
Pierce, Harvey W., 59-60
Pike's Peak Gold Rush, 9
Pinos Altos, New Mexico, 99
Pircher, Louis, 29
Pitkin County Railroad, 37
Polar Star building, 85
Polar Star Mill, 22, 24, 27, 64
Porter Bell & Company 0-4-0 tender locomotives, 11, *14, 15*
Potter, Thomas H., 37, 106
Pray, Col. E. E., 37
Prize Mine, 37, 85
Prosser Curve, 59
Prosser Gulch, 63
Prosser Gulch bridge, *58, 60-61*
Public Sampling Works, 19, 48

Quartz Hill, 11, 24
    Newhouse Tunnel, 62
    Slaughter House case, 19
    "The Patch," *38-39*
Quartz Hill branch, 67
"Quartz Hill" locomotive. *See* Shay 3 locomotive

Rail, 91
Randolph, Col. George E., 62
Randolph Mill, 22
Redaskey, A. H. and M. S., 65
Register building, 10
Register-Call, 28, 40
Richardson, Robert W., 85
Richmond, Dr., 24
Rickard, [Mr.], 40
Rio Grande Southern Railroad, 48
Rocky Mountain News, 28, 48
Roderick Dow Mine, *38*
Rogers, Andrew W., 19
Rogers, Fred N., 65
Roundhouse Curve, 45
Russell brothers, 9
Russell Gulch, 10, 25, 40, 63
    abandoned mines, *88*
Russell Park, *34-35*, 40, 41

San Juan Mine, 41
Saratoga grade, 85
Saratoga Mine, 29
Saratoga Mines, *32, 33*, 62

Saratoga vein, 63
Section hands' pay, 64
Sensenderfer residence, 21
Shay 1 locomotive ("Gilpin"), *21, 23, 26-27*, 48, *50-51, 54-55, 65, 99*
    accidents, 24, 30
    arrival in Black Hawk, 21
    sold, 62, 91
    used for Black Hawk yard trackage, 59
Shay 2 locomotive ("Russell"), *28*, 48, *50-51, 54-55, 56, 68-69, 99*
    accidents, 41, 59
    description, 24
    design, *94*
    excursion, 40
    ore hauled, 40
    put into service, 24-25
    repairs, 41
    sold, 62, 91
    used for mainline, 59
    used with snowplow, 40
Shay 3 locomotive ("Quartz Hill"), *38-39, 42-43, 44, 46-47*, 48, *49, 50-51, 54-55, 68-69, 76, 77, 82*
    accidents, 41, 58-59, *60-61*
    arrival in Black Hawk, 40-41
    conversion to 3-foot gauge, 98
    design, *95*
    ore hauled, 59
    scrapped, 98
    size of shipment, 45
    used for mainline, 59
Shay 4 locomotive, 62, *76, 77, 98*
    accident, 64
    conversion to 3-foot gauge, 98
    scrapped, 98
Shay 5 locomotive, 62, *68, 72-73, 74, 75*, 91
    conversion to 3-foot gauge, 98
    design, *96*
    scrapped, 98
Shinner, Zeck, 41
Silver City, Pinos Altos & Mogollon Railroad, 62, 91, *99*
Silver City, New Mexico, 99
Silver Plume, 81
Simmons and Clark, 25
Slaughter House case, 19
Sloan, R. E., 62
Smith Lode, 9
Sneckman, Charles, 41

Snow
    equipment for removal, 64, 76
    removal, 64, *66-67, 67*
    tracks blocked, 40, 62
Snowplows, 64, 91, 100
Springdale Mine, 45
St. Louis-Gunnell Mine, 45, 48
Starck [engineer], 24
Steele, W. C., 29, 34
Stock speculation, 9
Streeter & Lusk, 106
Sutro Tunnel, 63

Tabb, Jimmy, 45
Tabor, H. A. W., 48, 106
Teller House, 10
Thompson, James V. (Jim), 28, 48, 50, *50-51*
Tierney, John, 64
Tippett & Liberman Pool Hall, 48
Tippett, Charles P., 48
Topeka Lode, 45
Topeka Mill, 67
Tourtelotte Park, 37
Tramway Nine, 34, 41
Transfer, *87*
Turney, Jack, 45

Union Pacific, Denver & Gulf Railway
    agreement with Gilpin Tramway, 45
    and Colorado Central, 45
    takeover by Colorado & Southern Railway, 59-62
    shipments to Denver smelters, 48
    stations, *52*
Union Pacific, Denver & Gulf 2-8-0 locomotive, *17*
Union Pacific Railroad Company
    alleged interest in Gilpin Tramway, 28
    and Colorado & Clear Creek, 11
    and Colorado Central, 11, 22
    and Kansas Pacific and Denver Pacific, 11
    and Utah & Northern Railway, 21
    mainline, 11
    source of Porter Bell locomotives, 11
    telephone service, 48
    Tramway repairs, 59
Utah & Northern Railway, 21, 91

Virginia Tram Railroad Company, 106

Water Car 300, 48
Water transport, 48
Weekly Register-Call, 65

Wells, William A., 106
West Frontenac Mine, 40
Western Railway, 45
Williams, E. H., 40
Williams, Dan, 59
Winnebago Hill, *31, 41*, 62, *73*

Wrecks. *See* Accidents
Wye, 85

Yankee Hill & Western Incorporated, 106